HARD
Sayings

HARD
Sayings

Reconciling the Cost of Discipleship and the American Dream

JOSHUA WEST

AMBASSADOR INTERNATIONAL
GREENVILLE, SOUTH CAROLINA & BELFAST, NORTHERN IRELAND

www.ambassador-international.com

Hard Sayings

Reconciling the Cost of Discipleship and the American Dream

©2020 by Joshua West

ISBN: 978-1-62020-711-6
eISBN: 978-1-62020-735-2

Cover Design and Typesetting by Hannah Nichols

AMBASSADOR INTERNATIONAL
Emerald House
411 University Ridge, Suite B14
Greenville, SC 29601, USA
www.ambassador-international.com

AMBASSADOR BOOKS
The Mount
2 Woodstock Link
Belfast, BT6 8DD, Northern Ireland, UK
www.ambassadormedia.co.uk

The colophon is a trademark of Ambassador, a Christian publishing company.

Dedicated To:

Jesus Christ, my Savior, who sought me and bought me through the power of His shed blood on the cross. All glory to King Jesus.

To my dear friends and spiritual parents, Pastors Chad and Jennifer Burton, through whom I came to know Christ.

Pastor Dennis King through whom I was given my first opportunity to be a minister.

Pastor Edwin Lipsey whose love for the lost forever shaped me, and who has done more for me than I could ever say here.

To my friend, brother, and partner in ministry, Rev. Loren Shreffler. I could never fully express the impact you have had on my life and ministry.

To the ministries of the 180 Center and Sonrise Adult & Teen Challenge, through which I broke free from the bondage of addiction and learned what it means to truly be a disciple of Christ.

Last but definitely not least, my beautiful wife Kiara. You are my sunshine and you are my song.

FOREWORD

I consider Joshua West's book to be one of the most powerful prophetic writings of any other book currently on the market. His message to the church, if heeded, would bring correction to those who are neglecting to preach the full gospel message. In many pulpits the messages are intended to make the listener feel good about themselves rather than give forth a convicting word of repentance from sin. Preachers used to seek to convict sinners of their sin, instead of today too often neglecting to preach against sin.

Joshua writes in the style of my brother David Wilkerson's prophetic writings. As I read *Hard Sayings* I found myself beginning to underline portions to later review but then stopped; there are just too many power points to do so.

Joshua may or may not know it, but he has written a blockbuster of a message to the church and to preachers that preach from what I call a thin Bible; they leave out portions of the Word to accommodate the culture, the flesh, and worldliness. To those preachers and parishioners who buy into today's feel-good messages, reading *Hard Sayings* might be difficult, but Joshua writes with compassion, grace, and brokenness. May this book go farther into our culture than we thought.

—Don Wilkerson,
President
Teen Challenge, Inc
Brooklyn, N.Y.

CONTENTS

If anyone comes to me and does not hate father and mother, wife and children, brothers and sisters—yes, even their own life—such a person cannot be my disciple. And whoever does not carry their cross and follow me cannot be my disciple.

Luke 14:26-27 (NIV)

INTRODUCTION

I am a simple preacher of the gospel with a burning zeal for God's Word who has been called to preach a message of repentance to a church that has fallen asleep. First of all, let me start by saying that I am not an authority on anything. There are many men of much greater intellect and ability who write books on theology and doctrine such as C.S. Lewis, A.W. Tozer, and St. Augustine of Hippo. I am grateful for their insight and ability to illuminate the weighty things of God's Word for a simple man like myself. I am a student of Scripture and theology and a grateful benefactor of these men's works. However, I have a deep concern about the churches in America and it's a concern that I cannot shake. Our churches are slowing drifting off course and I don't think that I am the only one who senses this. Actually, in light of what is true, neither my feelings, nor anyone else's matter. Truth is not defined by what we feel; truth is truth despite our feelings, and God is God despite our feelings.

As I set out to write this book I immersed myself in the Scriptures and tried to divorce myself from any concepts or ideas about Jesus' teachings and what it means to be Christian that are not directly found in Scripture. This is not an easy task. From the time we are born we begin to form our view of the world and of God. My goal was to present a view of Jesus Christ and Christian discipleship strictly from God's Word. Within the American Christian culture, there is a version of Jesus that has emerged that is much different than what the Scriptures reveal. As I honestly and openly search the Scriptures, I've found some places where it is hard to reconcile Christian culture and the American church to what the Bible teaches. I struggle with this. I am not trying to say I've discovered special information, or that I know some deep mystery that is unavailable to anyone else. Far from it. I merely wish to clear away any view of Jesus and what it means to follow Him that is not firmly established in the Scripture.

It is human nature for us to deceive ourselves and form a view of Christ or discipleship that is easier to accept, or that aligns with our culture. What we should do is hold ourselves accountable to the truth no matter the cost. I know this sounds like a novel idea, but the fact that we will fall short isn't a reason not to try. If we truly believe the Bible, we know that one day we'll be held accountable to the truth as revealed in God's Word, by the person Who *is truth*, Christ Himself.

This book is not a Christian apologetic in the strictest sense. What I mean is this book is not aimed at people who would wholly deny the existence of God. (But if an atheist were to read it, I hope that they would at least find it informational.) This book is written to challenge our Americanized perception of God and Christianity. It is written with the assumption that the reader believes in God and the authority of Scripture, even though they may have different perceptions about what that means.

My hope is to undo the mythical Americanized Jesus that has been created in our minds by Western secular and Christian culture, and to paint a picture of the Biblical Jesus using history as my canvas and Scripture as the brush. I hope to define what it means to be a Christian from the words of Scripture and not what we have made it here in the Western world.

We live in an increasingly post-Christian society and the only way back is to rediscover the person and purpose of Jesus as revealed in the Scripture, and to come to terms with what it truly means to be one of His disciples. Some of what is being taught in America today seems to have been pasteurized and made more palatable for mass consumption. We believe we can take anything and make it better. While that may be true in other areas, the gospel must be the exception. If we will subject ourselves to the Scriptures and allow ourselves and our churches to be led by the Spirit, we'll be able to live in a way that builds up the Kingdom and brings glory to God.

WHERE I STARTED

Before becoming a Christian, I lived a pretty wild, reckless, and wicked life. I found a way to be rebellious in nearly every circumstance. I lived life on my terms and I took pride in that fact. If there was an anthem for my life it easily could have been Frank Sinatra's song, "My Way," but doing it your way isn't always glamorous like a song and rarely turns out like it does in the movies. Being reckless and wild had its price and in the year 2000, I spent nearly a year in jail for violating the probation I was serving. While in jail, I was confronted with the gospel and the hard sayings of Jesus from another inmate who had a Bible study in the cell-block I was in. He got me to begin reading my Bible and praying. But he was sort of extreme; he acted like this Christianity thing was an all-or-nothing proposition. Although he challenged me and I learned a lot from him, he seemed to be caught up in this legalistic concept that Jesus wanted us to lay down our lives for Him, die to ourselves, and live life as God's servant, which didn't interest me all that much. I wanted the Jesus the televangelists preached about, the one who wanted to bless me and make me great, the one who wanted everyone to be rich and happy. Once I got out of jail, I went back to my old ways. Although I was still drinking and doing drugs, I did wonder about God sometimes and found myself drawn to the Scriptures. I began reading the Bible and watching televangelists on late night television, but it was confusing because what I read in the Bible didn't really seem to reconcile with what many of these men where saying on TV. I chalked it up to the fact that I was new to the Bible and that they probably had better insight than I did. I liked what they were saying because most of their preaching was about becoming rich and being blessed which sounded pretty good to me.

In 2001, I visited a church called Living Word Global Church whose pastor was named Chad Burton. Pastor Chad was a very calm and humble man, very well educated and knowledgeable of the Bible. He didn't shout or yell like many of the televangelists did—he just preached straight out of the Bible and went through it in order like it was a story or something. He would stop and break down each part contextually and what he preached made so much sense; I would later learn that this was called expository preaching. Although he didn't yell, he was very passionate, and his words seemed to have authority and power. In fact, many times I would leave feeling bad about the life I was leading outside of church, but then I would realize he was wrong because I would hear a sermon on television that would remind me that no one is perfect, and that God was in the blessing business and wanted me to be happy. The only problem was, I wasn't happy. Pastor Chad was a great guy and very kind, but I began to believe that he wasn't very spiritual (or so I thought) because what he was saying seemed to contradict what the TV preachers were saying. I thought to myself, "Pastor Chad is well-meaning and nice, but I guess he doesn't have the same anointing or spiritual depth of these great men of God. Chad's church is small, and these men have huge world-wide ministries; these men are rich and successful and Chad seems to be content pastoring this small group of people."

But something always troubled me—everything about Chad's life seemed sincere and real. He cared deeply about the people in his congregation like they were family, and he preached the Scriptures like every word mattered. The only problem was he didn't seem to want greatness and that was what I wanted more than anything else. I wanted Christianity to open the door to my biggest dreams, I wanted faith that could move any mountain that stood in the way of my greatness and success. Chad was very approachable, so I began to ask him questions about what he preached and when it didn't line up with what I thought, he always pointed me to Scripture, not to himself. He was very patient and began to explain the gospel of Jesus Christ to me.

One Sunday morning I was in church after having consumed my weight in liquor the night before and Pastor Chad read these words out of the book of Matthew: "Whoever wants to be my disciple must deny themselves and take up their cross and follow me. For whoever wants to save their life will lose it, but whoever loses their life for me will find it" (Matthew 16:24-25, NIV). I was blown away that these words were in the Bible and that Jesus said them. How did the TV preachers preach what they did? Either they didn't know this was in the Bible or they did, which was something much worse. I realized that living for God was something that I wasn't going to be able to do "my way." I came forward at the end of the service weeping, and I surrendered my life to Christ. Shortly after this, Pastor Chad started teaching a series on the parables of Jesus and they blew my mind. I began to realize that nearly every preconceived notion about who Jesus was and what He taught that I had was wrong.

Chad became my pastor, mentor, and dear friend. He loved a very selfish and unlovely sinner to the cross, without compromise or veering from the truth. He would always quote the Apostle Paul and say, "there is no formula—only the truth presented in love." The most important gift Chad gave me besides leading me to the Lord was that he taught me that no matter who is saying it, if it doesn't reconcile to the Scriptures, it is wrong. He taught me to fear the Lord, love the Scripture, and that the gospel preached through the power of the Holy Spirit is enough. To this day there is no pastor whom I respect and admire more than Pastor Chad Burton. Much of what Jesus teaches us in the Scripture is very hard for us to accept because it is completely contrary to our human nature and the desires of our flesh. But if we truly believe that the Scripture is inherent and inspired by God's Holy Spirit, we will disregard anything that doesn't reconcile itself to the Bible no matter who says it or how good it looks or sounds.

EVALUATING THE TASK AT HAND

We could never come close to completely understanding God. I could write a hundred books and not cover all that needs to be said about Jesus, His teachings, and what it means to follow Him. Humans do not have the capacity to fully know God. We can't know everything, but we can know what God has chosen to reveal to us in the Scriptures, through the Spirit, and through study of the life and person of Jesus Christ.

It is with great honor toward the Lord, and with humility, that I set out to write this book. This book will be flawed just like any work touched by human hands, but my goal is to draw you closer to Jesus and the Scripture, not to myself. My goal in this book is to challenge the reader to re-evaluate his or her cultural perception, and the lens through which Jesus is viewed. We should always be working and growing toward viewing Jesus and the Scripture from a proper biblical perspective and context. The Scripture should be the scale upon which we weigh every concept's value and truth.

As I sought the Lord in writing this book, and thought about the task at hand, I was overwhelmed. This is by no means an exhaustive summary of Jesus' teachings, the Person of Christ, or an exhaustive guide to true discipleship. That book has already been written—it's called the Bible. The point of this book is to ask hard questions such as can we reconcile the teachings of Jesus with the American dream, and what do we do with the parts that don't fit?

I wept over the American church as I wrote parts of this book. My heart breaks for many preachers who preach broad-road theology and feel-good messages in their efforts to grow the church, rather than being Spirit-led and fearless, preaching the gospel, and letting Christ build His church. We must remember that anything we build with our hands, no matter how big it gets, is void of the power of the Spirit. It is incapable of drawing anyone to the Lord. It's only when the true gospel is preached, and we lift the name of Jesus high in accordance to His Word, that the power of the Spirit will empower us. We are here to do God's will, not our own.

CHAPTER 1

MARKETING AN AMERICAN JESUS

Being born in the United States is like winning the lottery compared to the conditions in which most people of the world live. Even the poorest among us are more blessed than the majority of people in places like India and much of Africa. We have great access to food, water, and the basic necessities required to survive. No one walks miles to get water or waits for bags of rice to be dropped off by relief workers. We have more food in our dumpsters than many people have in their houses in third-world countries. America is known around the world as the land of opportunity. People come here from all over the world to find a better life.

In the Declaration of Independence, it says that Americans have three unalienable rights: life, liberty, and the pursuit of happiness. It doesn't promise happiness, but it does give the right to pursue it, which is a blessing in and of itself. Yet one in five Americans are diagnosed with depression and according to the CDC (Centers for Disease Control and Prevention), the suicide rate in the United States is up nearly thirty percent since 1999. We are the most prosperous society in history, so if wealth could buy happiness we should be the happiest country in the world. But that is far from the truth.

We are drowning in a sea of excess and trying desperately to find meaning in our post-Christian society, and as a result, have become consumers of the highest order. Americans are exposed to scores of commercials trying to sell us everything from insurance to prescription medication. Announcers point out the holes we have yet to fill in the landscape of our American dream and remind us of our desperate need for their products. Souls are being lost one life-changing cleaning product and one high-tech gadget at a time.

We have allowed truth to be systematically undone and reason to be suspended for our convenience and entertainment. Yet we boast ourselves as a Christian society. The Pew Research Center found in 2014 that a little more than seventy percent of Americans identified as Christian. But if we are a majority Christian culture, then how can we explain the legal murder of sixty-one million unborn babies in our country since 1973? Much of the pro-life movement is reduced to an abortion regulatory system; a talking point that politicians use as campaign rhetoric. The murder of babies merely for the sake of convenience is a clear example of a culture gone mad. We are so selfish that we would rather destroy life than take moral responsibility for our actions and the consequences they bring.

We talk about sexual freedom out of one side of our mouth and then seem confused by the onslaught of sexual diseases, unwanted babies, and broken homes. Abortion is not the only godless thing about our society, but it is a great example of the sheer insanity of a culture that counts the miracle of precious life as an inconvenience. There are more people on waiting lists to adopt than there are abortions every year, but we would rather murder a baby to cover up our sin and indiscretion, than save a baby's life and bless a family that cannot conceive. Pro-choice is a lie. It is better called what it really is—survival of the fittest. In this case, the innocent party never gets a choice. The choice to murder is made by the people whose primary duty in life should be to protect the child—the parents.

So, let's talk about sexual immorality in America. What is sexually immorality, and who talks like that anymore? Fornication is generally an accepted lifestyle today in our country. Living together before marriage is not only accepted but encouraged. I understand people who are not Christians living as they please, but many within the church see no problem with people who are living in sin being allowed to serve and hold leadership positions in the church.

Homosexuality is also being propagated to us through every avenue possible; in politics, through the media, and even by certain church denominations. And when you stand up for what's right and true, you are called judgmental or a bigot.

So, what about the church? The Bible says there will always be a remnant, a true church, but what is the temperature of the modern evangelical church here in America? Post-modern, subjective, and lukewarm. The American church has been rocked to sleep in the arms of *cultural relevance* and *tolerance*.

What does it mean to be a disciple of Jesus in this modern era? If the so-called *Emergent Church* is right, and biblical truth evolves with the cultural landscape of the day, then maybe I am overreacting. But if this is true, then how do we know which way is true north? Or is the value of direction as unimportant and outdated as the archaic concept of absolute truth? If subjectivism is true, then how can we know it? Because if nothing is absolute then that statement undoes itself.

What value could the outdated teachings of a first-century rabbi named Jesus have for a highly evolved and scientific world like ours? Probably not much unless He was, and is, everything He claimed to be in the Scriptures. But how could the hard sayings He spoke be understood in a literal sense in this day and age—many of which we are unable to reconcile with our notion of fairness, our so-called rights, and the all-important American dream. Jesus' words are not always that hard to understand, although they can be hard to accept when we are desperately trying to reconcile them to our wants and desires.

Many people who criticize the teachings of the Bible say that they don't agree with much of what the Bible says, but they do like the teachings of Jesus because He taught only about love and grace. Unfortunately, that isn't true. While Jesus did teach about the love of God and loving our fellow man, He also taught about things like hell, final judgment, and the dangers of money. We are consumers and we are used to being catered to. We're used to picking and choosing what we want and what we don't want. So why would the teachings of Jesus, or how we live, or how we worship, be any different?

We find ourselves in a diluted time in the American church. Many claim to believe in Jesus, or say they are Christians, but what this means varies greatly from person to person. One of the main reasons for this disparity is biblical illiteracy. Knowing the Scripture doesn't make you a Christian, and that isn't all there is to having true relationship with the Lord, but is does tell us what it means to have a relationship with the Lord. It tells us that God is revealing Himself to us to make Himself known. Without sound doctrine as found in the Scripture we can make *following* Jesus mean whatever we want it to mean. Not only does that not make logical sense, it's simply not true.

NOTHING IS SACRED

I was sitting in a waiting room for an appointment. As is now common in most waiting rooms, the television was on and it was showing an adult cartoon. In this cartoon it portrayed a figure that looked like the devil and another character who was obviously supposed to be Jesus. The Jesus character was wearing a diaper. After a short amount of dialogue, it became apparent that in this show Jesus and the devil were in a homosexual relationship. The show went on mocking Christ while the devil in the show heaped insults on Jesus and made Him look like an idiot.

A man in the waiting room with me seemed to think this representation of Jesus was quite humorous. He evidently noticed the look of absolute shock and disgust on my face and asked, "Is this show bothering you?"

I hadn't realized my feelings were so apparent, but I said that I was a Christian and that I loved Jesus and that I believed in Him for my salvation. I expressed that watching Him mocked in that way made me sad. It seemed the perfect opportunity to share my faith.

His reply shocked me. However, it's a clear example of the state of our country. He told me not to be so judgmental, then went on to explain that he was also a Christian and that he thought people like me gave Christians a bad name.

"It's just a television show so what does it matter?" he said. He went on to tell me his beliefs about Christianity. He said that if I really understood the love and grace of God that I wouldn't be bothered by things like this, and that God wasn't judgmental so I shouldn't be either. He concluded by saying that nobody's perfect and that God wants us to enjoy our lives.

I wasn't judging the man, but I wondered how someone who had truly experienced the saving grace of Jesus Christ could ever think it was funny to see Him mocked? How could someone who loved Jesus with his whole heart not weep at how that adult cartoon had portrayed Him? How could anyone who is a student of the Bible, and believer in the Trinitarian God, not tremble with fear at the thought of standing before God one day and explaining why that was funny to us?

This man's understanding of grace was obviously flawed, and so was his view of Jesus. In just the plainest of terms, I couldn't imagine showing that amount of disrespect to someone I didn't care for, much less the Savior of the world who had made such a costly sacrifice for me.

This sort of irreverent representation of Jesus is becoming more common in our culture and is not only gaining more acceptance by those outside the church, but also by those who call themselves Christians. We should be careful not to over-generalize people; for instance, we must be careful when we use terms like *the church* or *American Christians* because there are many in those groups to whom this analysis doesn't apply. I am merely making a statement about cultural shifting that is plain for anyone to see.

It seems in an effort to make an unapproachable God approachable, some have twisted the grace of God into lasciviousness so that we can reconcile the person and teachings of Jesus to our fleshly desires, our sinful lifestyle, and the American dream. But there is only one thing that could ever make the unapproachable God approachable, and that is the precious blood of Jesus shed on the cross for our sins. The love and grace of God does cover our sins, but why would someone who truly loved and served Jesus, and realized that He is worthy of all our praise, ever enjoy watching Him be mocked?

Let me be clear about what I mean when I use the term the *American Dream*. I am talking about the desire to chase your dreams, have a large house, a nice car, and more than enough money in the bank. I am not saying that these things are necessarily good or bad; what I am saying is that just because something is promoted in American culture doesn't mean it's right according to the Scripture. It is our duty as Christians to examine everything according to the Scripture. What Jesus taught in Scripture should be the framework by which we strive to live our lives, not what American culture says is acceptable. Culture shifts and changes, but Christ is unchanging. He is the same yesterday, today, and forever.

Today bumper stickers, T-shirts, and media, make Jesus out to be some sort of pop culture hippy surfer. Marketing shapes much of our perception in life; unfortunately, how our culture represents Jesus is no different. We shouldn't let our view of Jesus be shaped by movies, marketing, and commercialized church propaganda. Jesus was fully man and fully God. He came in humility in order to save us. Not because He was simple or weak, but because He loved us.

One of the greatest problems we have with understanding the person of Jesus is we tend to see Him, His teachings, and the gospel through an American lens. Jesus isn't a hipster white guy from the suburbs. Jesus was born to a Jewish girl in the first century and His earthly father was a working-class carpenter. To understand the Bible and the teachings of Christ, we must first understand the culture in which it was written. You don't have to be a theologian to be a Christian, but we should, at the very least, give as much attention to studying and understanding the Bible as we do secular history.

Study to shew thyself approved unto God, a workman that
needeth not to be ashamed, rightly dividing the word of truth.

2 Timothy 2:15 (KJV)

We must do our best to understand how Jesus' teachings were understood
by a first-century audience instead of a twenty-first century audience. Like
most of us, I have been guilty of reading the Bible and explaining away the
things I didn't understand, as well as the things that I was unwilling to accept.
A lot of the content of Jesus' teachings are hard to reconcile with our modern
culture of excess and debauchery.

Let's be clear. If Jesus is truly God incarnate, although we should strive
to learn and apply everything His word says to our lives, we must also accept
the fact that there are some mysteries about the Trinitarian God our human
minds simply cannot understand. This doesn't mean we shouldn't seek Him.
God is Spirit and He desires to have a spiritual relationship with each one of
us. Although we can never have a complete knowledge of God, we can know
what God has chosen to reveal to us through nature, in our hearts and minds,
but mostly from the sacred Scriptures which is the lens through which we
should view the other two.

Oh, the depth of the riches of the wisdom and knowledge of God!

How unsearchable his judgments,

and his paths beyond tracing out!

"Who has known the mind of the Lord?

Or who has been his counselor?"

"Who has ever given to God,

that God should repay them?"

For from him and through him and for him are all things.

To him be the glory forever! Amen.

Romans 11:33-36 (NIV)

Since our free society is capitalistic, and less and less bound by any ethical restraints, the lengths to which we are willing to go to market our products are ever increasing. Sadly, to much of the church, Christianity and the person of Jesus are just another product. The goal of marketing is to make something seem appealing so that people will be attracted to, and accepting of, whatever it is we want them to buy. The message of Jesus, although given to us out of a spirit of love, isn't a marketing campaign to get you to like Him. It is a bridge leading us away from the consequence of our sin and into eternal fellowship with the Lord. So why do we make Jesus out to be something He is not? Because maybe it's not Jesus we are trying to draw people to, maybe it's ourselves! We want to fill our churches with people, we want to sell our Christian books, and many within the American church are willing to go to nearly any length to accomplish these.

CHAPTER 2

LAODICEA, AMERICA

In the book of Revelation, the Apostle John documents the words spoken to him by the resurrected Christ which, in part, are given to us in the form of letters to seven different churches. The tone of each letter is different. Some are letters of encouragement to a persecuted church which, despite adverse conditions, had held fast to the truth without wavering. Some are full of rebuke and calls to repentance for hollow churches that have lost their way, while others are a sort of a mix of encouragement and correction. One of these letters is addressed to the Church in Laodicea. This letter has a harsh tone and, in my mind, paints a picture similar to the state of the modern evangelical church in America.

To the angel of the church in Laodicea write:

> These are the words of the Amen, the faithful and true witness, the ruler of God's creation. I know your deeds, that you are neither cold nor hot. I wish you were either one or the other! So, because you are lukewarm—neither hot nor cold—I am about to spit you out of my mouth. You say, 'I am rich; I have acquired wealth and do not need a thing.' But you do not realize that you are wretched, pitiful, poor, blind and naked. I counsel you to buy from me gold refined in the fire, so you can become rich; and white clothes to wear, so you can cover your shameful nakedness; and salve to put on your eyes, so you can see.
>
> Revelation 3:14-18 (NIV)

The church of Laodicea, spoken about by Jesus in Revelation 3, was a church in Asia-Minor, which is now modern-day Turkey. It was near the church in Colossae with which it was apparently in fellowship. This is made clear from the fact that the church of Laodicea is mentioned several times in the epistle to the Colossians and Paul commanded the Colossians to pass the letter to the Laodiceans once they had read it.

By all accounts, the Laodicean church was a healthy church, filled with affluent people. Through the rebuke of Jesus, we see that their wealth had blinded them to the fact that they were spiritually bankrupt by comparison. Worldly riches are meaningless in contrast to spiritual riches. The things of this world are rapidly passing away while spiritual treasures endure forever. There is no amount of wealth that is worth your eternal soul

> For what shall it profit a man, if he shall gain the whole world, and lose his own soul?
>
> Mark 8:36 (KJV)

Although the message Jesus gave to the Laodicean church was a message for a particular church at a particular time in history, the message and lessons given there, as with most of the Bible, can be applied elsewhere. The letter to the church of Laodicea should serve as a warning for the American church. A church that makes a home in a culture that is obsessed with personal wealth and prosperity can be a church less concerned with sound doctrine and more lukewarm. Preaching about holiness is called legalism, standing up for the truth in the midst of culture is called judgmental, and preaching the full counsel of God and calling the lost to repentance has become an obstacle to church growth.

I'm not saying that there are no God-fearing, God-serving churches in America. I'm saying that American church culture as a whole seems to be resembling the description of the church talked about in Revelation 3:14-18. We feel comfortable because of our worldly wealth, but spiritually we are wretched, pitiful, poor, blind, and naked.

Why doesn't this frighten us or at least cause us to examine ourselves? It's because we have been conditioned over time to believe that examining ourselves is wrong, or at least unnecessary. Many believe that examining ourselves somehow undermines the grace of God. But, honestly, without examination of self we will never understand our need for grace—the grace extended to us in salvation and the grace we need in order to walk out our faith from day to day.

> Examine yourselves to see whether you are in the faith; test yourselves. Do you not realize that Christ Jesus is in you—unless, of course, you fail the test?
>
> 2 Corinthians 13:5 (NIV)

As disciples we must be disciplined. We must learn what Jesus expects of us as His disciples. As sinners we were cold and so were our hearts; dead in our sins and separated from God. Once we are reborn in Christ we become full of passion, full of life, and full of love that comes from God alone. So, what's so wrong with being a little less than hot? Say, maybe *lukewarm*?

LUKEWARM OR TRANSFORMED

There are two points of view about the passage in Revelation 3 where Jesus says, "I wish that you were either hot or cold but since you are lukewarm I am about to spit you out of my mouth." I have heard it preached that God wants us to be hot which is being in right relationship with Him. But He would rather us be cold, which is to be completely out of relationship with Him, than for us to be lukewarm, which is to think we are in relationship with Him when we are not. At least those who are cold know they are in need, whereas the lukewarm person thinks everything is all right when actually, they are headed for destruction.

The other perspective is that in the context of the verse, both hot water and cold water are good for something, but lukewarm water is good for nothing. Hot water is good to cook with and to wash and clean with, while cold water is refreshing to drink. I tend to think the second view probably makes more sense contextually and logically. Either way you look at it, it's true from both perspectives. Lukewarm is good for nothing, and those who are lukewarm will be spit out of Jesus' mouth.

What is a lukewarm Christian? In my opinion there's no such thing. The Scripture says that He will spit the lukewarm from His mouth; He never says they are Christians. We tend to assume He is addressing Christians because this letter is written to a church, and like many evangelicals today, we believe that because people are in church they're Christians. We use the term *lukewarm* when we talk about Christians who have lost their fire, or Christians who have lost passion, or someone who is going through a stagnant season. In other words, Christians who aren't on fire for God. But in the context of Revelation 3, Jesus is speaking to a person who seems like a Christian but really is not. The reason I believe this to be true is that Christianity is not performance-based, but rather evidence-based. Either you are a Christian or you are not. Listen carefully to the words of Jesus regarding detecting the evidence of true Christianity, or as He says, "the fruit" of someone who is truly a disciple of His.

> A good tree cannot bear bad fruit, and a bad tree cannot bear good fruit. Every tree that does not bear good fruit is cut down and thrown into the fire. Thus, by their fruit you will recognize them.
> Matthew 7:18-20 (NIV)

Good fruit, good works, and the way a Christian lives, are outward evidence of an inward transformation of someone who has been made alive in Christ. It's evidence of the fact that Christ is living in them and through them. Performance-based Christianity means if you don't do enough good works, you're not a Christian, or that you're a lukewarm Christian because you didn't try hard enough or didn't give enough.

Make no mistake—true Christians will do good works, not to obtain salvation, but as *evidence of salvation*. God will spit the lukewarm and false converts out of His mouth one day. Those who are not sons and daughters of God and disciples of Jesus, will be separated from those who are.

For we are God's handiwork, created in Christ Jesus to do good works, which God prepared in advance for us to do.

Ephesians 2:10 (NIV)

American culture is aimed at consumerism and comfort, and somehow we have let that become part of the church as well. If the power of the Holy Spirit is moving and alive in our churches we don't need gimmicks. When all our adoration and worship is aimed at Jesus, the Holy Spirit is there with us. Instead, what we have is a prosperity gospel, a social gospel, and celebrity preachers whose doctrine is shaky at best, pursuing what God can provide instead of a passion and zeal for God Himself.

Celebrity pastors (many of whom live in a way that mocks God and looks no different than the world) preach messages that contradict one of the primary messages of Jesus: "Repent for the kingdom of God has come near." With no conviction about anything, and no position on anything, they clamor for the spotlight and the approval of man. Hiding behind a paper-thin concept of love and a twisted view of grace, they stay neutral on every important issue because they're too afraid speak the truth. This is lukewarm at its core. They hide their cowardice by saying they are *seeker-friendly*.

The transforming, resurrection power of Christ living inside of a person is a fire that cannot be contained; it burns with passion and sets other things on fire. Even when a fire is small, or it begins to wane, it still cannot be considered lukewarm, because even a small fire will burn you. If you touch even the tiniest of embers you will be burned. A true Christian cannot be lukewarm. A true Christian can, however, lose passion and let their flame dwindle down to small flame or even an ember.

The difference between the struggling or weary Christian and the false convert is this: the lukewarm or false convert will be spit out of His mouth, but a true Christian's flame will not be extinguished. When we struggle as children of God He does not want to extinguish us or snuff us out. He wants to fan the flame inside us back into a raging fire. God wants to nurture and build us up into the image of Jesus so that we can endure until the end and forever be with Him.

> *A bruised reed he will not break,*
>
> *and a smoldering wick he will not snuff out,*
>
> *till he has brought justice through to victory.*

Matthew 12:20 (NIV)

Jesus didn't come to snuff out the flames of His people, He came to empower them with His grace. Unfortunately, many people are expecting to receive grace from a God they haven't accepted, through a Savior they don't know. God's grace is for His people. Now God does extend a common grace to all mankind. This is evident by the air in our lungs and life that we live. Even sinners who hate God enjoy a common grace that they refuse to acknowledge, but all the things in the earth and in our lives that sustain our lives come from God.

God didn't create us for survival; He created us for communion and fellowship with Him. Although all are blessed with God's common grace, it is our choice if we want to partake in His amazing grace—His saving grace that comes only in a life surrendered to Him.

It's all or nothing. Either we are His or we are not. It's through true belief in Christ that we are saved, not just knowing about Him. So what is true belief?

What if I told you that I would buy you a brand-new car and it would cost you nothing? A brand-new car with all the bells and whistles, right off the assembly line. The only condition is that before I buy it, you must find someone who needed a car and give the car you already own to them. Your car is old and barely running, but you need your car to get to work and to take care of

31

your family, so giving your car away would seem sort of foolish, right? Unless, of course, I was going to buy you a brand-new car, no strings attached. What reason would you have to not give your car away? It comes down to one of two things; either you truly didn't want the brand-new car that I was offering because you liked your old one, or you didn't trust me to keep my word. This is the sort of belief required to be saved. I'll explain.

Giving up your old car shows that you truly believe that I will keep my word, and your actions prove it. Not that your action has anything to do with your salvation, but your action validates that you do believe. Trust is the starting point of a real and intimate relationship, and without trust, you don't have an intimate relationship. Many people who are so-called lukewarm Christians are just false converts who haven't even begun to have a relationship with God because they are unwilling to have faith in Him. It is impossible to please God without faith.

> And without faith it is impossible to please God, because anyone who comes to him must believe that he exists and that he rewards those who earnestly seek him.
>
> Hebrews 11:6 (NIV)

We cannot base the security of our salvation on what we feel or what we want. Wanting something badly cannot change reality. Don't confuse wanting something badly with faith. Faith is a knowing or expectation that God will keep His word. Faith is trusting that we are justified before God through the atoning work of Christ Jesus and that He will keep His promises and fulfill His will in the earth.

JESUS, MY PERSONAL SAVIOR?

For those who claim to be in Christ, there are many misconceptions about the person and teachings of Jesus. This is not referring to actual scholarly debates where men and women who are true students of the Bible have differences of opinion about various points of theology, or have different interpretations of what small portions of Scripture mean. I'm referring to the gross mischaracterizations about the person and message of Jesus as found in the New Testament.

Let me put it another way. How could we ever paint Jesus in such a way that is nowhere found in the Scriptures? It is actually simple. Many people within the American church don't study the Bible for themselves. We would rather listen to a smooth-message preacher feed us something that validates what we *want* to hear, not what we *need* to hear.

Following Christ is about discipleship, which has a lot to do with discipline and correction. This is what the word *disciple* means. When a sinful man begins to be discipled and transformed by a perfect God everything must change. This isn't legalism, it's transformation. We know our lives are lacking; we know deep down that we are lost without His grace. Why then do we buy into a brand of Christianity without transformation, repentance, and self-denial? It may be because we are lazy and we want things to be as easy as possible, so to accomplish this we have turned God's grace into lasciviousness.

We keep lowering the bar of what it means to follow Christ, and we do it under the banner of grace. But in order to pervert what grace is, we have to pervert who Jesus is and what He taught. The Bible is clear about what Jesus taught. It runs countercultural; it goes against your feelings. It's uncomfortable and it costs everything you have. It truly is laying down your old life and taking on an entirely new life and nature. But I have to add—it's worth it. It's worth whatever the cost.

The Scriptures command us to live in a way that pleases God, but the Spirit *enables* us to live in a way that pleases God. Not only does God want to help us walk this out, but it is impossible to do it without Him. It's not trying harder to do better, it's surrendering more and more each day. As we give up the places of our heart that once served as idols to sin and self, our obedience makes room for the Spirit's power in our lives.

We market Jesus as someone who wants to be our *personal Savior,* which can be misleading. I fear this has created a version of Jesus that is far from the biblical reality. Saying that we can know Jesus individually and personally is a true and a needed message; but this is sometimes presented in a way that communicates that Jesus will shift and change to accommodate our desires and our preferences. Personal Savior for some means that Jesus is our customer service representative and is here to make our Christian experience more comfortable and enjoyable. Jesus is the King of Kings and Lord of Lords and to view Him in any other way is extremely foolish.

> For those God foreknew he also predestined to be conformed to the image of his Son, that he might be the firstborn among many brothers and sisters.
>
> Romans 8:29 (NIV)

Those who are born of God must be conformed to the image of His son. A personal relationship with Jesus means we conform to His image; He will never conform to ours. Jesus is perfect in every way and beautiful in every way, and we are called to let Him change us from the inside out. He is the firstborn from the dead, and we are literally adopted into the family of God when we surrender our lives to Him. The problem with the whole idea of saying a prayer one time in the back of a church and asking Jesus to be our personal Savior is that it isn't a true call to follow Jesus. It is not a real presentation of the gospel.

> Whoever does not take up their cross and follow me is not worthy of me. Whoever finds their life will lose it, and whoever loses their life for my sake will find it.
>
> Matthew 10:38-39 (NIV)

"Whoever loses their life for my sake will find it?" This doesn't sound like what many are preaching today:

Jesus wants to empower your life! Jesus wants to prosper your life with material stuff! Jesus wants you to dream big and He will make all your dreams come true if you follow Him!

That doesn't sound much like "Whoever does not take up their cross and follow me is not worthy of me." The cross was the ultimate symbol of death and shame; this, my friends, is a call to die. A call to die to one's self and follow Jesus with no guarantees except for the fact that we are saved by His grace and that one day we will see Him face to face. And if you really know Jesus, you know that's enough.

The teachings of Jesus aren't just wise sayings of a sage, teacher, or rabbi, instead they are the very wisdom of God as revealed in the God-man Jesus Christ. We can never forget that the teachings of Jesus are the wisdom of God the Father and God the Holy Spirit. To discount or minimize any of Jesus' words is to blaspheme God. We must be deliberate in our effort to understand what Jesus intended when He spoke in the Scriptures and try to not superimpose our agenda or westernize or modernize the message.

It does not matter how big our buildings are, how many people attend our church, or how much social change we affect in our community. If we are lukewarm and without faith that produces deeds, then we are without God and we are building nothing but piles of hay, wood, and stubble that will be burned up on the day of judgment.

CHAPTER 3

IMAGE OF THE INVISIBLE GOD

In the beginning was the Word, and the Word was with God, and the Word was God. He was with God in the beginning. Through him all things were made; without him nothing was made that has been made. In him was life, and that life was the light of all mankind. The light shines in the darkness, and the darkness has not overcome it.

John 1:1-5 (NIV)

There is no way to exaggerate the importance of Jesus. Thousands of songs have been written to honor Him, and we could write thousands more and never exhaust the reservoir of beauty that is Christ. He is the Creator of the universe. He is the answer to all things because He is the origin of all things. He is the centerpiece of life, because He is the author of life. He is the creator of time, God of the universe, and the Savior of the world.

Mental assent, or mere theological knowledge, isn't what God desires from us. He wishes to have us for His own; this is why He created us. Although it is relationship that God desires from us, we have to make sure our view of that relationship is based in the reality and truth of Scripture. People seeking God from experience only run the risk of falling into deception. Experience that doesn't line up with Scripture isn't from the Spirit. Anything that can't be reconciled to Scripture is probably just emotion and from our flesh. On the other hand, it is possible to amass knowledge of the Scripture and never experience fellowship with God. It has much to do with our motives and intentions.

When I was a young boy, I remember singing songs in church that spoke of the glory of Jesus and His majesty and power but having no idea what I was saying. I mentally believed that God was real, but I never put much thought into it. It certainly wasn't important enough to influence my decisions, or the way I led my life.

As I grew older, I fell away from the church and deep into sin. I realize now I had always been full of sin, but as a teenager and a young adult I saturated myself in an atmosphere that nurtured that sin. I lived my life as if there were no God. It's ironic that after I was consumed by addiction and despair, I blamed the God Whom I had ignored most of my life for what had become of my life.

When I was a boy I was told that if I prayed a little salvation mantra at church that I would be covered as long as I really meant what I had recited. I was told that I should live for God and that He loved me and wanted me to live for Him. At least if I said the prayer I was going to heaven either way.

Fast forward many years later. I had lived a selfish and self-gratifying life and now I found myself in the Lew Sterrett County Jail in Dallas, Texas, serving a nine-month stretch for violating my probation. One day while serving my time, another inmate asked me if I was a follower of Christ. I hesitated to answer because no one had ever asked me that before. I responded by saying that I hadn't lived for God but that I was a Christian. Then he asked, why did I think I was a Christian? I didn't know how to respond. Then he asked me why I thought I could be a Christian without being a follower of Christ. I was stunned, I didn't know what to say.

I explained that although I had some ups and down that I had accepted Jesus in my heart as a boy and that I said the salvation prayer and that made me a Christian. He asked me to show him in the Bible where it said that.

I poured over the New Testament for the better part of two days so I could put this guy in his place, but came up with nothing. At first, I was upset with him. I thought, this guy doesn't know anything about God's grace, but I did respect the fact that everything he said came from the Bible. He seemed to burn with a passion and love for God and it seemed important to him to share this with me.

He began to present the gospel to me from the Scriptures and it seemed different than the altar calls I was used to. I argued with him and regurgitated a flawed and unbiblical doctrine of grace I had heard from celebrity preachers on Christian television. Their messages had comforted me in my sinful lifestyle, but never seemed to have the power change anything.

He told me that I should read the gospel of Mark, and after that the book of Romans. I began to read through Mark, but my heart was so hard it didn't faze me much. I read it and skipped over a lot of it because I thought to myself, "I already know all this stuff." This guy also told me to pray that God would reveal Himself to me through His Word before I read the Bible. So I did.

One day while lying on my bunk in my cell I began to read the book of Romans and something about it reached out and grabbed me. Not just my attention, but something deeper. For the first time ever, the Scripture began to speak to me. My eyes were opened and for the first time I saw it all. I read that God's wrath was being stored up for those who live a lawless life and that a day of judgment awaited all who lived this way. I started to feel a sense of worry inside and a feeling of conviction came over me because I knew it was talking to me. I realized that I deserved God's wrath and punishment. But as I read on I saw and understood for the first time what grace was and what Jesus had truly done for me on the cross and that I desperately needed Him for salvation.

> The Son is the image of the invisible God, the firstborn over all creation. For in him all things were created: things in heaven and on earth, visible and invisible, whether thrones or powers or rulers or authorities; all things have been created through him and

for him. He is before all things, and in him all things hold together. And he is the head of the body, the church; he is the beginning and the firstborn from among the dead, so that in everything
he might have the supremacy. For God was pleased to have all his
fullness dwell in him, and through him to reconcile to himself all
things, whether things on earth or things in heaven, by making
peace through his blood, shed on the cross.

Colossians 1:15-20 (NIV)

I read through the New Testament several times over the next few
months and it was during this period that I read Colossians 1:15-20 and it
stuck with me. It says so much. Christ is above all things and He literally
created all things that are seen and unseen. There is nothing in the entire
universe that is outside of Him, nothing that is before Him. I had always
thought of God as the Father and Jesus just as His son. I never truly saw
Christ as God until then. He is before all things and in Him all things hold
together. Even now as I ponder this, my mind explodes with all the implica-
tions and possibilities of this statement. All things were created through
Him which I felt I understood, but it also said all things were created for
Him and I guess that included me.

In one moment, every hymn I had ever sung came to life; all the Bible stories I'd ever heard meant something different than I had once thought. I realized that this life that I couldn't manage or find meaning in hadn't worked
because it wasn't made for me. It was made for Him and *I was made for Him.*

It wasn't purpose that I needed to seek after, it was Him. He is everything and in Him is everything. Jesus Christ is the image of the invisible God.
Everything the Godhead wanted us to know about the person and character
of God, He revealed to us in the person of Jesus Christ. Everything hinges on
Him; creation, prophecy, salvation, resurrection, and eternity. The entirety of
Scripture is wrapped up in the person of Christ. He was there in the beginning, but He Himself has no beginning. He is the focus and dividing line

of time, although He Himself is not subject to time. He created time and is eternally above it and beyond it, although He chooses to interact with us in it. Jesus is the King of Kings and Lord of Lords and it is from a place of complete sovereignty and complete authority that He enters the landscape of human history. But for what? To redeem a people that He can call His own!

So, when we do anything to undermine Him, His power, or His word to make people feel comfortable, we blaspheme Him. What right do we have, as servants of the King, to edit the message that He has sent us to deliver? If you were a messenger, or a servant of a king, and he sent you on a journey to deliver a message he wrote to someone else, and you edited it or changed it because you were worried about how it would be received, you wouldn't be a very good messenger. You would possibly be put to death for high treason, or be put in prison as a traitor, but at the very least you would be considered a bad servant to the king. By your actions you would be doing a couple of things.

First, you are misrepresenting the king. Who are you to alter what he is saying? Is your place above his?

Second, you are doubting the wisdom of the king and in the case of Christ we are saying that somehow the creation has insight or wisdom that the Creator does not. This truly is foolishness.

THE WORD REVEALED THROUGH THE WORD

The second person of the trinity, Jesus Christ, spoke the world into existence and is God, along with God the Father and God the Holy Spirit. In the first chapter of the Gospel of John, we get a glimpse into the creation story from a different perspective than we get from Genesis 1. John attributes the origin of all things to Christ. John is showing that although Jesus was born into humanity by a virgin girl in the first century, this wasn't His true beginning; He has no beginning and no end. Jesus Christ is the example and visual representation of God on earth.

The Holy Spirit, through the writing of John, reveals Jesus as Messiah and as God. The culmination of all prophesy, all history, and all creation hinges on the person of Christ. This why we cannot flippantly portray Jesus in any way that is not supported in the Scripture. If we believe that the Scripture is the true and inspired Word of God, then why wouldn't we carefully weigh our view of Christ, the gospel, and eternity on Him? Although we are indwelled by the Spirit of God if we are truly saved, we must remember that it is easy to let our emotions and our flesh mislead us. We must, therefore, reconcile ourselves to the Scriptures because the Holy Spirit of God will never contradict the written Word of God because Jesus is the Word.

It is not only foolish, but it is dangerous to view Christ in a way that doesn't line up with the Scripture. So much of what is said about Jesus in our culture today is not biblical and because of this, we have allowed a view of Jesus into the church that is passive and accepting of everything. When culture is contrasted to the picture of Jesus painted in the Gospels and the picture of God in the Old Testament, something much different emerges.

The message of Jesus in the New Testament isn't any different than the message of the prophets in the Old Testament because they are the words of the same God—a God who never changes. To think that the God of the universe, who created time, would bend His will to change just because of the modern culture is not only a small view of God, but it is also heretical in sight of what the Scripture teaches. The message of repentance for the sake of salvation is a common thread throughout the Bible and has never changed. The only difference between the repentance message the prophets spoke of and the repentance message Jesus spoke of is that when Jesus spoke it He said, "Repent for the kingdom of God has come near." He was the long-awaited Messiah, literally the essence of heaven walking on the earth. Also, this spoke of the actual Kingdom which His life, death, and resurrection would set into motion: A Kingdom that He would rule for all eternity.

John records an interaction between a teacher of the law named Nicodemus and Jesus in the third chapter of his Gospel. Like the teaching found later in Luke 14:25-27, what He tells Nicodemus is equally intense. In this section in Luke, Jesus teaches about the radical cost of discipleship and He says that we should hate father, mother, sister, brother, and even our own lives, and that we must deny self, pick up our cross, and follow Him.

> Jesus replied, "Very truly I tell you, no one can see the kingdom of God unless they are born again.
>
> John 3:3 (NIV)

All men are born of water, but to take on the nature of Christ we must be born of the Spirit. So being a disciple isn't just abandoning an old way of life and taking on a new one, it is to put to death an old nature and to be reborn into a brand-new nature. This is why people who are not reborn in the Spirit have such a hard time understanding what Jesus asks of us. It is in conflict with our sinful nature and is impossible to do without the internal transformation that comes from the work and indwelling of the Holy Spirit.

This is a problem I have with much of today's preaching. Out of desperation to explain the unexplainable, we devalue the worth and mystery that makes up the transformed life of the spiritual man and the vastness of the triune God. There is a lot of reasonable evidence in science, nature, and logic to use in a balanced Christian apologetic. But as A.W Tozer would put it, "To describe God's function isn't to explain Him philosophically." We truly show how little we understand spiritual things when we think that we can fully explain the supernatural God of all creation through and by natural causes.

I believe that we should study the Scripture deeply and intently. Not to amass theological knowledge, but to hear from God Himself and to know Him from His own living words. We spend a lot of time trying to explain God instead of spending time adoring God. A person who has no preconceived notion of God will have a much easier time experiencing God's Word and discovering the person of Christ in that Word. The obstacle of belief is not only the adding of truth, but it is also the removal of lies.

Most have been influenced by lies and misconceptions about God, ourselves, and about the world. For the most part you are the product of whatever your environment dictates unless something from the outside intervenes. Your view of reality is greatly influenced by your culture: where you were born, how you were raised, and what you were taught. For example, there are cultures that are taught hatred for other cultures from birth and then spend their lives despising those groups of people. If they were not taught to hate from birth, they would probably have no problems with this hatred. This is why when we are born again everything must be reconsidered in view of the cross and everything must be reexamined in light of the Scripture. Our greatest teacher and example is Jesus Christ who is God and also our Savior.

> Philip said, "Lord, show us the Father and that will be enough for us." Jesus answered: "Don't you know me, Philip, even after I have been among you such a long time? Anyone who has seen me has seen the Father. How can you say, 'Show us the Father'? Don't you believe that I am in the Father, and that the Father is in me? The words I say to you I do not speak on my own authority. Rather, it is the Father, living in me, who is doing his work. Believe me when I say that I am in the Father and the Father is in me; or at least believe on the evidence of the works themselves.
>
> John 14:8-11 (NIV)

All we need to know about God is revealed to us in Christ. To see Jesus is to see God, to know Jesus is to know God, and to be in Christ is to be justified before God on the basis of faith. Jesus wasn't merely a messenger, or a prophet; He is the image of the invisible God and the person of the Godhead that God the Father chose to endow with all power and authority. Jesus is the dividing line between true worship and false worship, true Christianity and cults. The truth about everything in this life, in this world, and in the universe must be judged on its ability to reconcile itself to Jesus Christ. Jesus doesn't merely possess or fully comprehend the truth, rather He is the truth, He is light, and He is life. We could write books from now until the end of time and never come close to exhausting those concepts or fully grasping the majesty, wonder, and power of the truth of Jesus Christ.

CHAPTER 4

FALSE CONVERTS AND TRUE DISCIPLES

Enter through the narrow gate. For wide is the gate and broad is the road that leads to destruction, and many enter through it. But small is the gate and narrow the road that leads to life, and only a few find it.

Matthew 7:13-14 (NIV)

Have you ever considered what it means to follow Jesus? What if you did this: reconsider all the perceptions you grew up believing, all the traditional understanding you have (based on the church in which you grew up), your denomination's positions on things, what your parents believed, what your pastor (or anyone else for that matter) had taught you. What if you re-examined everything you believed about being a Christian from Scripture alone?

If you have never attempted this exercise, you should, because this is the standard by which you will be judged. Until we have a true encounter with Christ in which we repent for our past, surrender our future, and let the Holy Spirit take up residence in our lives, we will never be able to perceive spiritual things. We must make sure that what we say and preach about salvation through Christ, and about who the person of Jesus truly is, lines up with Scripture. If we do not, we're not only deceiving ourselves, but we may be deceiving others as well.

Several years ago, I started feeling a burden in my spirit and conviction in my heart for the complacency that God began to reveal in my life. Not a complacency about how much I was giving or my level of dedication to the ministry, but the degree to which I let popular church culture dictate what was right and wrong, what was acceptable and what was not, instead of the Scriptures. Many of these things are subtle and creep in over time, but I began to see that I had an overly *Americanized* view of the gospel with regard to what it truly means to be a disciple of Jesus.

When we take the Scriptures and the words of Jesus at face value and don't use Americanized logic and our culture of ease and comfort to explain away the hard sayings of Jesus and the true cost of discipleship, we are left with something much different than the gospel of accommodation we hear from many pulpits today. I began trying to divorce the Scripture from my own cultural bias, the bias I had gained by living my entire life in America. I also began to try to sort through "church sayings." These are the things you hear people say in church that sound spiritual and almost biblical but are not actually in the Bible. I cast those aside. Everything must be reconciled to the words of Scripture.

So much of what Americans believe is built around a view of convenience and comfort rather than self-denial and laying everything down at the foot of the cross. We are responsible for what we believe, and we are responsible to study the Bible for ourselves. The Scripture should have the final word on everything.

Do you think most people are going to be saved? What in the Scripture leads you to think that? The sort of casual association with Jesus many people who claim Christ in America have doesn't reconcile with the dramatic and life-changing encounters of Jesus' disciples and true saints throughout church history. The disciples walked away from everything they knew to follow Jesus. Matthew left his tax collector's booth. Peter, Andrew, James, and John left behind the security of their family's fishing businesses. Paul left behind his life as Saul the Pharisee. All throughout the history of the church, people have been forsaking worldly riches and security to follow Jesus. Even to this day Christians throughout Asia, Africa, and the Arab world choose to follow Jesus despite the great personal cost that they may incur for being a Christian. This is about becoming a disciple of Jesus, a follower, a servant, not saying a prayer in the back of a church that you don't even understand. Doesn't it bother us at all that the framework most churches use to lead people to Christ, is void of repentance, surrender, and the gospel as presented in the Scripture?

The teachings of Jesus say something different than what much of the American church says. The mainstream and the status quo might not be good enough to offer the true security of salvation. We are obsessed with talking ourselves into believing that our lost loved ones and friends are somehow saved because they attend church, or are good people by society's standards, or because they grew up in a so-called Christian home—even though it's obvious their lives are not bearing fruit.

I'm not saying this to be cruel. I'm saying this so that we feel the needed sense of urgency to pray for them and preach the gospel to them instead of living in denial about the state of their souls. The Scripture says, " . . . broad is the road that leads to destruction, and many enter through it. But small is the gate and narrow the road that leads to life, and only a few find it" (Matthew 7:13b-14). When we look into the crowds of the megachurch do we assume that most of the people sitting in the seats are *all right with God?* Is there even such a thing as being *all right with God?* Is there such a thing as lukewarm Christians? Or casual Christians? Or are most of them walking down a broad road that is paved with easy answers, comfort, compromise, and headed straight for hell?

It is interesting that rarely do we hear sermons about false converts when so many of the parables of Jesus address that very topic. But not just in parables—Jesus is straightforward with this message in Matthew 7. Here He addresses false converts directly.

> "Not everyone who says to me, 'Lord, Lord,' will enter the kingdom
> of heaven, but only the one who does the will of my Father who
> is in heaven. Many will say to me on that day, 'Lord, Lord, did we
> not prophesy in your name and in your name drive out demons
> and in your name perform many miracles?' Then I will tell them
> plainly, 'I never knew you. Away from me, you evildoers!'
>
> Matthew 7:21-23 (NIV)

It's striking that Jesus doesn't say that you are exempt from this message if you repeated a salvation mantra in church at some point. In fact, the way most people attempt to present the gospel is nowhere to be found in Scripture. Inviting Jesus to come into your life without the willingness to follow Him and lay down everything is not salvation, it is self-deception. So much of what Jesus says to us through the Scriptures were words of warning. Why do we preach about salvation as though it is about the words we say, rather than a choice to give up an old corrupt nature and life, and take on an entirely new nature and life?

Where is the urgency? Do we really believe all things outside of Christ are subject to judgment? Do we think that people who have repeated a half-hearted prayer in church are going to be saved from the wrath that is to come? Why do we think that God will suffer a people who do not fear Him, respect Him, or have a casual association with His Son who bled and died for us? We know by the thief that hung next to Jesus on the cross that it's not about a life well lived. Obviously, the thief didn't have time or opportunity to even bear fruit as far as works go, but he did bear the fruit of repentance due to a moment of wisdom that came from fearing the Lord. Let's examine the components of his conversion.

> One of the criminals who were hanged there was hurling abuse at
> Him, saying, "Are You not the Christ? Save Yourself and us!" But
> the other answered, and rebuking him said, "Do you not even fear
> God, since you are under the same sentence of condemnation?
> And we indeed are suffering justly, for we are receiving what we

deserve for our deeds; but this man has done nothing wrong." And he was saying, "Jesus, remember me when You come in Your kingdom!" And He said to him, "Truly I say to you, today you shall be with Me in Paradise."

Luke 23:39-43 (NASB)

The fear of the Lord and repentance of sin seems to be what motivated the thief who Christ said would be with Him in paradise. He was aware of his sin and his need for a savior. If the salvation offered by Christ is one given on the basis of faith, what might have caused the thief who was repentant to have faith in Christ? I believe it was in response to the words of Jesus when He prayed for the very people who were insulting Him and abusing Him, "Father, forgive them; for they know not what they do." This must have brought conviction to this man's heart knowing that Jesus was being crucified the same way he was although He had done nothing wrong. Instead of being angry or resentful, Jesus cried out for God to forgive those who had hung Him there. We should have the same reaction when confronted with the fact that a Holy God would die on our behalf, especially when we deserve the wrath of God, not the mercy of God.

> The fear of the Lord is the beginning of wisdom, and knowledge of the Holy One is understanding.

Proverbs 9:10 (NIV)

I believe that one of the reasons the church is full of false converts is because somewhere along the way we removed repentance from the gospel and we no longer preach the fear of the Lord. Salvation occurs when a sinner becomes aware of God and His perfect law of justice, and then feels conviction for their sins. It's the conviction of our sin that leads us to repentance. This is where faith comes in. If we believe like the thief on the cross that Jesus' death took our place and took our rightful punishment, then we can accept the free gift of salvation. Before you truly can accept forgiveness, you must first acknowledge your sin; you must acknowledge your need for forgiveness. If we were not truly desperate sinners deserving of judgment and on our way to hell, then why do we say that we are *saved*? If we were not sinners deserving of wrath, then Jesus died for nothing.

Another reason so many false converts think they are saved is because we offer something the person wants and tell them that they will receive it if they follow Jesus. But here's what you actually get when you follow Jesus. You get *Jesus*. If that statement isn't enough for you, you are probably not truly one of His.

> . . . that if you confess with your mouth the Lord Jesus and believe in your heart that God has raised Him from the dead, you will be saved.
>
> Romans 10:9 (NKJV)

What does it mean to follow Jesus according to the Scripture? I can tell you this: it has little to do with reciting a salvation mantra that you don't believe. The so-called salvation prayer isn't magic. Confessing with your mouth and believing in your heart doesn't mean that if you conjure up the courage to recite a prayer that some magic in that prayer will save you. If you believe that God raised Christ from the dead, of course, you will confess it. You will preach the gospel everywhere you go, because that's what true converts do. The term *Christian* in our culture doesn't mean much anymore, so that's why I use terms like "servant of Christ," "Christ follower," or "disciple." These present a clearer statement than *Christian*. Many people in the West call themselves Christians, but they don't follow Christ like a true disciple or servant.

THE COST OF DISCIPLESHIP

People seem confused by the idea that there is a cost to following Jesus. Phrases like "suffering for Christ," "laying down your life," and "dying to self" are archaic concepts in the church that many in this modern, hyper-tolerate, purpose-driven, prosperity-driven age would rather not talk about. But I assure you that there is a cost to following Jesus. It will cost you everything. True belief comes in seeing the value of who you are laying your life down for. This is what it means to love God.

> "If anyone comes to me and does not hate father and mother, wife and children, brothers and sisters—yes, even their own life—such a person cannot be my disciple. And whoever does not carry their cross and follow me cannot be my disciple. Suppose one of you wants to build a tower. Won't you first sit down and estimate the cost to see if you have enough money to complete it? For if you lay the foundation and are not able to finish it, everyone who sees it will ridicule you, saying, 'This person began to build and wasn't able to finish.' Or suppose a king is about to go to war against another king. Won't he first sit down and consider whether he is able with ten thousand men to oppose the one coming against him with twenty thousand? If he is not able, he will send a delegation while the other is still a long way off and will ask for terms of peace. In the same way, those of you who do not give up everything you have cannot be my disciples.
>
> Luke 14:26-33 (NIV)

Those of you who do not give up everything cannot be my disciple! I am sure I have read over those words many times before in my life, quickly passing over them like many other passages that I didn't like or understand. But I remember the first time I saw that statement for what it meant and it pierced my heart. It cut through the foolish perception of Jesus I had allowed to be built in my mind by Christian propaganda. To follow Jesus, it would cost me everything I had.

Many people who are presented with the truth about what it means to follow Jesus reject it. Perhaps not openly, but in their minds they say, "Surely Jesus doesn't want me to suffer or give stuff up. That doesn't sound like the Jesus I know."

The question then is: who is the Jesus you know? The passage above is the Jesus of the Bible, the Jesus who spoke more about the subject of hell and final judgment than anyone else. The same Jesus who said, "It is easier for a camel to go through the eye of a needle than for someone who is rich to enter the kingdom of God" (Mark 10:25, NIV). The same Jesus who ate with sinners and died for sinners, and the Jesus who spoke about wealth like it was something to flee from rather than something to seek after. We are guilty in this day and age of marketing and focusing on the attributes of Christ we like and know are easy to receive by others. Much of the time we are dishonest in our silence about the parts we know the world will not agree with.

I understand the logic. Let's show people that God is love, and not talk about His perfect justice, His holiness, His call for *our* holiness, His wrath and judgment, and the requirement for us to lay everything at the foot of the cross. That way, by not revealing the whole character of God as shown to us, we get people in the doors of our churches. The problem is once we get them in the doors, we want to keep them, so we suppress the truth further in an effort to show God's love and over time we can win them over. Unfortunately, that doesn't work because until we admit our sin and turn from it, we are still dead in our sins. You can be as sensitive about it as you want; there is never a good time to tell someone they have cancer, and unless it's dealt with, they will die. Salvation is a call to come and die, to die to yourself.

I'm not suggesting that we be harsh or hateful, but just that we preach the truth. We have an amazing opportunity for evangelism across America. Seeker-friendly, entertainment-centered churches are full of people who desperately need to hear real, spirit-led, Scripture-centered preaching that will confront them with the truth about the gospel. False converts are people who claim faith in Christ but bear no fruit and are unwilling to deny themselves, or live their lives as a living sacrifice.

> Therefore, I urge you, brothers and sisters, in view of God's mercy, to offer your bodies as a living sacrifice, holy and pleasing to God—this is your true and proper worship.
>
> Romans 12:1 (NIV)

Living a life of sacrifice isn't anything that makes us special, exceptional, or great as Christians. It is, rather, evidence that you are in Christ and understand the need to live life in view of God's mercy. The worship of a true disciple is evident in their lifestyle more so than in singing along with worship songs at church. Offering our bodies as a living sacrifice is our true and proper worship. Anyone can get swept up in the moment during the worship set at a church gathering. The evidence of true-life transformation is validated by the way we live our lives.

Be sure of this: there is cost to be a disciple of Jesus. It will cost you everything and it's worth so much more than that. Because of His amazing grace and great love for us, He gave us something we don't deserve and that we could never earn.

PARABLES ABOUT FALSE CONVERTS

Many people today put the scriptural teaching on Hell in opposition to the love of God. But Jesus combines them. Here is an important truth: no one loves you more than Jesus Christ, and yet, no one spoke of or taught on Hell and judgment more than Jesus Christ. There is warning after warning, parable after parable, that speak, warn, and even shout judgment and the reality of Hell. Although some say that a God of love wouldn't allow eternal punishment in Hell, God's justice demands it.

Many people buy into a false version of Jesus and of salvation because it suits their lifestyle and their false notion of discipleship. If nothing changed in your life after you confessed faith in Christ, it's possible you aren't saved. Not because the power of Christ is lacking, but that you don't truly believe. True belief is proved true by action. Jesus spoke many parables on the topic of false converts. In the parable of the ten virgins, Jesus makes it clear that many who believe they will inherit life will not. I don't know about you but to me this is a thought that is frightening.

"At that time the kingdom of heaven will be like ten virgins who took their lamps and went out to meet the bridegroom. Five of them were foolish and five were wise. The foolish ones took their lamps but did not take any oil with them. The wise ones, however, took oil in jars along with their lamps. The bridegroom was a long time in coming, and they all became drowsy and fell asleep. At midnight the cry rang out: 'Here's the bridegroom! Come out to meet him!'

"Then all the virgins woke up and trimmed their lamps. The foolish ones said to the wise, 'Give us some of your oil; our lamps are going out.' 'No,' they replied, 'there may not be enough for both us and you. Instead, go to those who sell oil and buy some for yourselves.' But while they were on their way to buy the oil, the bridegroom arrived. The virgins who were ready went in with him to the wedding banquet. And the door was shut.

"Later the others also came. 'Lord, Lord,' they said, 'open the door for us!' But he replied, 'Truly I tell you, I don't know you.' Therefore, keep watch, because you do not know the day or the hour.

Matthew 25:1-13 (NIV)

There is no parable that shakes me to my core as much as this one does. Matthew 25 contains three parables: *The Parable of the Ten Virgins, The Parable of the Talents,* and *The Parable of the Sheep and Goats.* The reason this parable is so scary is that like in Matthew 7:15-20, it gives the sober warning that not everyone who claims to be in Christ is, and not everyone who thinks they are going to Heaven actually will.

In the ancient world, unmarried women did not have status or an equal place in society. The fact that these virgins or unmarried women were invited to a wedding ceremony would have been a great honor, and to not show up would have been a great dishonor. Five of these women were considered foolish and five were considered wise. What separated them? The answer is the wise were prepared with oil and the foolish ones were not. The idea of being prepared is the central point to many of Jesus' parables. In the chapter preceding this parable, Jesus gives a sober warning about this very thing.

"But about that day or hour no one knows, not even the angels in heaven, nor the Son, but only the Father. As it was in the days of Noah, so it will be at the coming of the Son of Man. For in the days before the flood, people were eating and drinking, marrying and giving in marriage, up to the day Noah entered the ark; and they knew nothing about what would happen until the flood came and took them all away. That is how it will be at the coming of the Son of Man. Two men will be in the field; one will be taken and the other left. Two women will be grinding with a hand mill; one will be taken and the other left.

"Therefore keep watch, because you do not know on what day your Lord will come. But understand this: If the owner of the house had known at what time of night the thief was coming, he would have kept watch and would not have let his house be broken into. So you also must be ready, because the Son of Man will come at an hour when you do not expect him.

"Who then is the faithful and wise servant, whom the master has put in charge of the servants in his household to give them their food at the proper time? It will be good for that servant whose master finds him doing so when he returns. Truly I tell you, he will put him in charge of all his possessions. But suppose that servant is wicked and says to himself, 'My master is staying away a long time,' and he then begins to beat his fellow servants and to eat and drink with drunkards. The master of that servant will come on a day when he does not expect him and at an hour he is not aware of. He will cut him to pieces and assign him a place with the hypocrites, where there will be weeping and gnashing of teeth."

Matthew 24:36-51 (NIV)

It is in light of this stark warning that Jesus delivers the parable of the Ten Virgins. The lack of preparation on the part of the foolish virgins shows their lack of care about the wedding banquet to which they have been invited. I am concerned that this is the state of many people sitting in churches all across America every Sunday morning. They have plenty of time to cultivate oil but never seem to get around to it. These people are false converts and will be surprised on the day that the bridegroom comes because they think that somehow they will be able to attend the wedding anyway.

This is why they say, "Lord, Lord, open the door for us," to which He responds, "Truly I tell you I don't know you." What a frightening thought, believing you are all right with the Savior and yet discovering on that day that your flawed knowledge of God wasn't enough to save you.

It's foolish to think you have a valid relationship with someone you don't really know and who doesn't know you in an intimate way. The words of Jesus make it clear that being prepared is important. If it were not, Jesus wouldn't have said it so many times. Don't confuse having knowledge of Jesus with having fellowship with Him.

Matthew 25:1-13 and Matthew 7:21-23 make it clear that many people who attend church, who serve in the church, and who feel that they are all right with God will not inherit eternal life. It's not enough to call Him *Lord*. Surrender of everything is what God wants; it's what He demands. We must come to the place where Christ becomes so real to us that nothing else matters. When we see Christ and the gospel for what it truly is, nothing standing next to it can measure up. The Apostle Paul understood this. He left behind social status, prestige, financial security, and comfort, but to him it was worth it. He literally viewed all of those things as garbage next to the beauty of Jesus:

> But whatever were gains to me I now consider loss for the sake of Christ. What is more, I consider everything a loss because of the surpassing worth of knowing Christ Jesus my Lord, for whose sake I have lost all things. I consider them garbage, that I may gain Christ and be found in him, not having a righteousness of my own that comes from the law, but that which is through faith in Christ—the righteousness that comes from God on the basis of faith.
>
> Philippians 3:7-9 (NIV)

Remember this though, giving stuff up or denying yourself in and of itself isn't discipleship. Fellowship with Christ is the point here. I didn't fall in love with my wife because she told me I had to give up dating other women and told me that she wanted me to live by a list of rules and boundaries. That makes no sense. When I first met my wife, I was still free to do as I pleased. I could see who I wanted to see and live life as I chose. However, after getting to know her, and after I fell in love with her and saw such an immense value in her, I wanted to marry her and entered into an intimate relationship. I chose to forsake all others and live as a married man with all the rules and boundaries associated with a healthy and Godly marriage. It was and is my great pleasure to do my best to live up the title of husband because my wife has my heart. I'm not a perfect husband but it's the desire of my heart to be; my love for my wife is not only expressed in word, but in also in my actions. Here's my question: as disciples, do we feel the same way about Jesus? Righteousness, or right standing with God—which is salvation from sin and final judgment and the ability to fellowship with God—is preceded by a knowledge or belief in Christ to the degree that Paul says it surpasses all things. Things that were once important to him and once considered valuable, now seemed like garbage in comparison with knowing Jesus.

Only God truly knows who are His, but He has made it clear to us what is required to be saved. The Scripture says that if you believe in your heart and confess with your mouth that Jesus is the Lord that you will be saved.

But the concept of *belief* can be manipulated to include many who don't truly love God and many who don't truly know God. The parable of the ten virgins makes it clear that there are many self-deceived among the numbers of *believers*. Not only should we want to be with Christ, but our lives should show this relationship in the way we live. Are we prepared and eagerly awaiting the return of our beloved bridegroom? Or is it an afterthought to us as we preoccupy ourselves with the spiritual infidelity of this world?

Another parable He put forth to them, saying: "The kingdom of heaven is like a man who sowed good seed in his field; but while men slept, his enemy came and sowed tares among the wheat and went his way. But when the grain had sprouted and produced a crop, then the tares also appeared. So the servants of the owner came and said to him, 'Sir, did you not sow good seed in your field? How then does it have tares?' He said to them, 'An enemy has done this.' The servants said to him, 'Do you want us then to go and gather them up?' But he said, 'No, lest while you gather up the tares you also uproot the wheat with them. Let both grow together until the harvest, and at the time of harvest I will say to the reapers, "First gather together the tares and bind them in bundles to burn them, but gather the wheat into my barn."

Matthew 13:24-30 (NKJV)

There will always be tares, or as other Bible translations say *weeds,* among the wheat crop. Just because you are growing next to wheat doesn't mean you are wheat. There will come a day when Jesus will judge things for what they actually are. He will harvest the wheat and the weeds will be bundled up and burned. This is obviously talking about true converts and false converts in the church. The fact that you're in the same field, and the fact that you're being allowed to grow, shouldn't bring you comfort or be the gauge by which you determine the surety of your salvation. Only those who have been transformed through Christ and bear the seal of the Holy Spirit will be saved.

It is possible to be surrounded by wheat and to be a weed. It is completely possible to hang around Jesus and still be lost. This fact is made clear by Judas Iscariot. He spent three and a half years in Jesus' inner circle and ended up not being one of His. He heard all the messages, teachings, and sermons. He witnessed many miracles, and saw prophecies fulfilled in the person and teaching of Jesus, but even then, he completely missed it. He chose to betray

Jesus. The Scripture actually says, in Judas' case, it would have been better for him if he'd never been born. Self-deception is powerful because our sin nature is powerful. Many people spend a great deal of time in and around church but are headed for Hell. This troubles me deeply. The thought of this has driven me to tears on more than one occasion.

Yet another parable that speaks about false converts and the day of separation when the Lord judges mankind, is the parable of the sheep and goats. It makes it clear that Christ Himself will judge mankind and will reward those who are truly His and send those who are not into eternal punishment.

> "When the Son of Man comes in his glory, and all the angels with him, he will sit on his glorious throne. All the nations will be gathered before him, and he will separate the people one from another as a shepherd separates the sheep from the goats. He will put the sheep on his right and the goats on his left.
>
> "Then the King will say to those on his right, 'Come, you who are blessed by my Father; take your inheritance, the kingdom prepared for you since the creation of the world. For I was hungry and you gave me something to eat, I was thirsty and you gave me something to drink, I was a stranger and you invited me in, I needed clothes and you clothed me, I was sick and you looked after me, I was in prison and you came to visit me.'
>
> "Then the righteous will answer him, 'Lord, when did we see you hungry and feed you, or thirsty and give you something to drink? When did we see you a stranger and invite you in, or needing clothes and clothe you? When did we see you sick or in prison and go to visit you?'
>
> "The King will reply, 'Truly I tell you, whatever you did for one of the least of these brothers and sisters of mine, you did for me.'
>
> "Then he will say to those on his left, 'Depart from me, you who are cursed, into the eternal fire prepared for the devil and his angels. For I was hungry and you gave me nothing to eat, I was thirsty and you gave me nothing to drink, I was a stranger and you did not invite me in, I needed clothes and you did not clothe me, I was sick and in prison and you did not look after me.'

"They also will answer, 'Lord, when did we see you hungry or
thirsty or a stranger or needing clothes or sick or in prison, and
did not help you?'

"He will reply, 'Truly I tell you, whatever you did not do for one of
the least of these, you did not do for me.'

"Then they will go away to eternal punishment, but the righteous
to eternal life."

Matthew 25:31-46 (NIV)

This is a perfect example of a hard saying of Jesus because it challenges our notion of fairness. It can cause some to question God's goodness. They might wonder how does one reconcile an all-loving God with eternal punishment? Let's start by understanding something. God is the creator of all things and He is sovereign, He is above all things and is subject to no one. Once we come to grips with this fact we start to understand that our notion of a so-called deserved fairness is flawed to start with.

God doesn't owe us anything. He is the *Creator*; we are the *created*. He can do what He pleases. If we view God through this lens we can finally understand and accept God's grace. What makes God's grace so truly amazing is that we do not deserve it and could never earn it.

Sheep are the ones who choose to follow Jesus. Goats, although they look similar to sheep, are not. They will be separated from those God calls His own. The parable almost makes it seem as though people who did good deeds will be saved because of their deeds. However, when read in the context of the entire Scripture, we see that the good works of the ones Christ calls His own, are merely evidence of their true nature. The book of James says it this way:

But someone will say, "You have faith; I have deeds." Show me
your faith without deeds, and I will show you my faith by my
deeds. You believe that there is one God. Good! Even the demons
believe that—and shudder.

James 2:18-19 (NIV)

Good works or deeds are not enough to save us, but they are evidence that someone truly believes. You can say you believe something, but if you say you believe but are unwilling to act, it shows that your so-called belief was empty words. In the parable of the sheep and the goats, Jesus is saying those who are in His will act like Him. When we surrender, accept, and choose to follow Christ, He transforms us and the evidence of that begins to show in the way we act, the way we treat people, the way we live. This doesn't mean that if you do good deeds you're a Christian because of it. Rather it points to the *evidence* that you truly believe.

There have always been false converts and there always will be until the day Jesus comes back to separate the sheep from the goats, the wheat from the tares, the foolish virgins from the wise virgins. But make no mistake, the day will come. This is why we must preach the true gospel, because without being confronted by the truth and without conviction, the lost will not be saved.

TRUE CONVERTS AND THE JOY OF SALVATION

When witnessing to people you have to dig deeper than merely asking, "Are you a Christian?" The term *Christian* means different things to different people. Many people will answer yes to this question without thinking twice. In Scripture we find two contrasting examples of different reactions to the opportunity at salvation. The first is the parable of the rich young ruler found in Matthew 19:16-30, Mark 10:17-27 and Luke 18:18-27. The second is the parable of the treasure in the field and the pearl of great price both found in Matthew 13:44-46.

The story of the rich young ruler is about a rich young man of great wealth who meets Jesus. In that brief encounter he asks Him the question, "What must I do to inherit eternal life?"

Scripture says that Jesus looked at him and loved him, and then proceeded to tell the young man what stood between him and eternal life. Jesus said, "Go and sell all you have and give to the poor and then you will have treasure in heaven, then come follow me."

What is odd is that the young man never asked about *following* Jesus, he merely asked what he must do to inherit eternal life. Jesus made it clear that it would cost him everything and that he would then have to follow Him.

Jesus didn't tell him to pray a prayer while no one is looking around, all heads bowed, and all eyes closed. He gave the man a loving, but firm, ultimatum. But because the man was wealthy and unwilling to give up his wealth, he went away sad.

Today, this guy wouldn't have gone away sad. We would have sworn him in as a deacon and put him on the financial committee. Jesus' reaction to the man didn't seem very *seeker-friendly*; but maybe we know better than He does about building the church. What is obvious is that this man saw more value in his life and what he had than he did in the person of Christ.

In Matthew 13:44-46, we see what a true convert's reaction to the gospel and the call of Jesus to follow Him looks like:

> "The kingdom of heaven is like treasure hidden in a field. When a man found it, he hid it again, and then in his joy went and sold all he had and bought that field.
> "Again, the kingdom of heaven is like a merchant looking for fine pearls. When he found one of great value, he went away and sold everything he had and bought it.
>
> Matthew 13:44-46 (NIV)

It says in the parable of the treasure in the field that when the man found the treasure, in his joy, he sold everything so that he could buy the field. Here lies the difference between the rich young ruler and the man who sold everything to buy the field. People who see Christ as a treasure will gladly give anything to obtain Him. This a far cry from how salvation is preached today, but we should be careful when weighing out these concepts, because eternity hangs in the balance.

THE NEW AMERICAN MISSION FIELD

What is one of the neediest places in America for the gospel to be preached? One place where the true gospel is in short supply but desperately needs to once again be preached is in many of our Evangelical churches, the American mega-churches, and the seeker-friendly churches. Those who are false converts fill the seats of these entertainment-driven, self-centered churches. They are comfortable and catered to. Most of those pastors are terrified that if they preach a hardline message against sin, or a message on holiness, or a message that focuses on the self-denial of the cross, people will leave the church.

There is no room to be a coward when you are a pastor. Being a pastor is about preaching the truth and being willing to help someone to see and know truth no matter what the personal cost might be. It's not about building a brand or an image, or even filling the seats. It's about being like the apostle Paul. You're so persuaded by the truth and so consumed by the gospel that nothing would stop you—not suffering, not persecution, not even death.

False converts are lost people. But they are more self-deceived than most lost people and we must reach them with the truth of the gospel. If this wasn't the case, then why did Jesus warn us so often about this issue? Why are so many parables and teachings of Jesus aimed at this particular group? Therefore, we must preach the *true gospel*—not a gospel of accommodation, not a seeker-friendly, or sin-accepting gospel, but the true gospel unedited and uncut.

It seems that many within the American church would rather keep the sanctuary full of people than preach like Peter did, like Paul did, and like Jesus did. Many pastors won't preach a message of repentance that says a tree that doesn't bear fruit will be cut down and thrown into the fire. But, this isn't a hostile message; it's a message of love and a message of truth. It's a message that says, "I care more about your eternal soul than I do about anything else."

CHAPTER 5

THE LEAST WILL BE GREATEST

Throughout the gospels, Jesus' disciples were jockeying for position and trying to set themselves up in positions of power in the earthly kingdom that they were eagerly waiting for Jesus to establish, despite the fact that time and again Jesus tried to explain that His Kingdom was first and foremost a spiritual one. Jesus wanted them to understand that the principles upon which His Kingdom was built were not the same as those of the temporal world.

We shouldn't be too hard on Jesus' disciples because we are no better. Much of Christian culture in the West today is wrapped up in a "kingdom now" theology and a "prosperity-centered" theology that is void of suffering, sacrifice, and service.

The true kingdom of God and the true character of Christ is laid out in the beginning of a message Jesus delivered in the book of Matthew which is referred to as the Sermon on the Mount.

> "Blessed are the poor in spirit, for theirs is the kingdom of heaven . . .
> Blessed are the meek, for they will inherit the earth . . .
> "Blessed are you when people insult you, persecute you and falsely say all kinds of evil against you because of me. Rejoice and be glad, because great is your reward in heaven, for in the same way they persecuted the prophets who were before you.
>
> Matthew 5:3, 5, 11-12 (NIV)

Basically, take everything that our culture strives for and admires, find the opposite, and you will have the teachings of Jesus in the Beatitudes. *Blessed are the poor in spirit, for theirs is the kingdom of heaven.* The poor in spirit, the lowly, and the humble are not what this world portrays as great and usually are not the ones who run the show. Most people, not all, but most people with wealth and influence did not get it by being humble or poor in spirit. You may achieve success by the world's standards in this life, but Jesus is saying that His Kingdom is built a different way, and it is a superior way.

What does it mean to be poor in spirit? Scripture gives several examples of men and women whom I believe meet this description. One of these was Abraham. Abraham had been promised by God that he would be the father of many descendants and nations and that the world would be blessed through him. Abraham and his wife were very old, and Elizabeth also happened to be barren. When they finally conceived a child after years of waiting, I can only imagine what that son meant to them. Isaac would be the heir and the fulfillment of God's promise in Abraham's life. Imagine what it must have been like when God told Abraham to take his precious son to top of Mt. Moriah and sacrifice him. Scripture doesn't describe Abraham's mental state or how great a struggle this had to have been for him, so I will not speculate, but we know in the end, Abraham obeyed God.

There is no doubt that Abraham loved his son—his son of promise—but he proved above all that he loved God more. He was willing to give up his prized possession in obedience to God.

Abraham took his son, placed him on the altar, and raised his knife to sacrifice Isaac. Before he went through with it, the Angel of the Lord said to him, "Do not harm the boy." Abraham looked up and saw a ram stuck in a thicket; the ram became the substitute sacrifice. God did not want the life of Isaac; He wanted to make sure that Abraham's prized possession, his son, did not have possession of his heart ahead of God (Genesis 22).

Moses is another example of someone who was poor in spirit. He rejected a place in the palace of Pharaoh in order to lead his people out of Egypt. If Moses had stayed in Egypt, he would have wanted for nothing. Instead, he obeyed God and traded a life of comfort for trial, adversity, and the unknown. Due to his obedience, God used him to free an entire race of people from slavery.

Poor in spirit is to be released from possession to the point that nothing or no one could ever come between you and God. This is the true worship of God. He must be first in all things and first in every part of your life. Anything less is idolatry.

Blessed are the meek, for they will inherit the earth. This statement was completely counterintuitive in the first-century as well as today. You wouldn't see meekness brought up in a training manual on how to be a power broker on Wall Street or to be the CEO of a major corporation. In fact, meekness is rarely looked at as a positive attribute in American culture. Only the strong survive in this world.

When Jesus said blessed are the meek and the poor in spirit, He cuts straight to the heart of what discipleship is all about. Those who are obsessed with material things will go to great lengths to show that it is possible to seek material things and still be blessed by the Lord. But this isn't the message of Jesus, nor does anything in the Bible bear witness to this. A greedy heart is blind and is willing to count any gain as blessing. Unfortunately, it's the millstone that is slowly tied to a conscience that will eventually be drowned by the weight of its own guilt.

> If any man teach otherwise, and consent not to wholesome words, even the words of our Lord Jesus Christ, and to the doctrine which is according to godliness; He is proud, knowing nothing, but doting about questions and strifes of words, whereof cometh envy, strife, railings, evil surmisings, Perverse disputings of men of corrupt minds, and destitute of the truth, supposing that gain is godliness: from such withdraw thyself. But godliness with contentment is great gain. For we brought nothing into this world,

and it is certain we can carry nothing out. And having food and raiment let us be therewith content. But they that will be rich fall into temptation and a snare, and into many foolish and hurtful lusts, which drown men in destruction and perdition. For the love of money is the root of all evil: which while some coveted after, they have erred from the faith, and pierced themselves through with many sorrows.

1 Timothy 6:3-10 (KJV)

A heart that desires material things has no problem inventing a theology to accommodate its greed; but to accomplish this the heart must ignore or deny much of the New Testament. No matter how much Scripture you show and how obvious the words of Jesus and Paul may be, the hardened heart will not listen.

Much of the American church is obsessed with trying to reconcile the gospel to the American dream of wealth, health, and worldly success. It seems many preachers believe if they have enough, or sow enough seed, they deserve God's blessing. But if you deserve something, it's not actually a blessing, is it?

Recently, I heard a famous preacher say that if you tithe as a Christian, God promises you a happy, successful, and comfortable life. I'm not sure where in the Scripture he gets that from, or what part of the teaching of Jesus makes him think that. In my estimation, Jesus never comes close to saying anything of the sort. Maybe that preacher has never read the words of Jesus in Luke 9:

As they were walking along the road, a man said to him, "I will follow you wherever you go." Jesus replied, "Foxes have dens and birds have nests, but the Son of Man has no place to lay his head." He said to another man, "Follow me." But he replied, "Lord, first let me go and bury my father." Jesus said to him, "Let the dead bury their own dead, but you go and proclaim the kingdom of God." Still another said, "I will follow you, Lord; but first let me go back and say goodbye to my family." Jesus replied, "No one who puts a hand to the plow and looks back is fit for service in the kingdom of God."

Luke 9:57-62 (NIV)

Jesus literally says to one man to follow Him and the man's response to Jesus is that he needed to take care of some family business first. He didn't want to go until his father passed away so he could be there to bury him. Seems like a noble reason, right? All of our reasons seem noble and important to us at the time, but when Jesus calls us to follow Him, it is an *accept Him* or *reject Him* moment. When one of them said, "I will follow you but first let me say goodbye to my family," Jesus said anyone who puts their hand to the plow and even looks back is not fit to serve in the kingdom of God.

God is much less concerned with our immediate and temporal comfort than He is with our obedience, our eternal soul, and for us to conform to the image of Christ. God's eternal Kingdom and a life in eternity in the presence of Jesus is our reward. Anyone who expects a trouble-free life or who thinks if we follow a certain preacher's biblical system or unlock certain secrets of the Bible, that we are guaranteed a comfortable life, is beyond deceived.

> "I have told you these things, so that in me you may have peace. In this world you will have trouble. But take heart! I have overcome the world."
>
> John 16:33 (NIV)

You will have trouble. Let me say that again, you will have trouble. Why? Because the true gospel brings trouble; it brings reproach by the world. Jesus didn't say that we should go looking for trouble, but preaching the truth and living a life of obedience to God in a culture that rejects His lordship will bring trouble. We are so terrified of people thinking that we are judgmental that many Christians would rather compromise the truth than endure persecution. We are comfortable talking about "servant leadership," but remove the word leadership and just say *servant*. Would you serve then?

Better is one day in your courts

than a thousand elsewhere;

I would rather be a doorkeeper in the house of my God

than dwell in the tents of the wicked.

For the Lord God is a sun and shield;

the Lord bestows favor and honor;

no good thing does he withhold

from those whose walk is blameless.

Psalm 84:10-11 (NIV)

David had a close relationship with God and although he was imperfect like we are—even made serious mistakes—he loved God and served God because of His worthiness, not because of what God would do for Him. Psalm 84 makes it crystal clear that David understood that to be with God and in His presence far exceeded being king of the entire world without God.

King David's life is a great example of this. When David was called to be king he was a shepherd and led an insignificant life. When the prophet Samuel told David's father Jesse to gather all of his sons because God was going to anoint one of them to be king of Israel, Jesse didn't even call for David.

It may have been because he was young or maybe it was because he wasn't a man of great stature. Either way, he was not included in the initial group of sons Jesse assembled before Samuel. He was definitely the least of all of his brothers. This story is found in 1 Samuel 16:1-13. In summary, David was anointed to be Israel's next king. However, right after he was anointed he went back to his flock of sheep.

David lived an insignificant life while being faithful to God, his family, and his role as a shepherd. Later, he would come to the forefront and slay a giant, but there were many years of serving under Saul, an earthly king who had been rejected by God. With meekness and faithfulness, David served. He did not pursue power; he did not try to force his way into the calling God had on his life. He served faithfully, trusting the Lord until it was his time to be king.

Jesus Himself is the greatest example of this. He lived in obscurity for thirty years until it was time to start His earthly ministry. Jesus did not seek personal greatness. Instead, He sought to fulfill the will of the Father and the task set before Him, which was to die on the cross. Personal significance isn't necessarily a bad thing if you are trying to fulfill the place in the body of Christ that He prepared for you to fill. Unfortunately, more often than not, people aren't trying to fill their place in the body; they are seeking personal greatness and selfish ambition and yet calling it the will of God.

THE BLESSING OF PERSECUTION

In Matthew 5, Matthew talks about the blessing of being persecuted for the sake of Christ and the kingdom of God. It's interesting to me that it never says "blessed are the blessed" or "blessed are the rich." But in order to prop up the notion that financial gain is godly we hear many preachers say this.

Instead, Jesus says, "blessed are those who are persecuted, blessed are the meek and blessed are the poor in spirit."

> Blessed are those who are persecuted because of righteousness, for theirs is the kingdom of heaven. Blessed are you when people insult you, persecute you and falsely say all kinds of evil against you because of me. Rejoice and be glad, because great is your reward in heaven, for in the same way they persecuted the prophets who were before you.
>
> Matthew 5:10-12 (NIV)

We should never look for validation or set the standard of our lives based on culture, even if that culture is so-called Christian. As we have witnessed in America over the last sixty years or so, culture will change. We should set the boundaries and standards in our lives from what God commands in the Scriptures not what is accepted by the masses. The rise of secular atheism and its open rejection of Christianity is at a level never seen before in this country. It has changed what it means to be a Christian at a social level. Open acceptance of sin, which was once looked down upon, has created an opportunity for the truth to shine in a way it hasn't before. Persecution forces us to reveal whether our convictions as a disciple of Jesus are genuine or counterfeit.

Christians are shown in the worst possible light in the liberal media, pop culture, and in academia in our country. Verbal disdain and criticism of Christianity is common. Not the feel-good, broad-road, encouragement-driven, purpose-driven, all-inclusive, life-coach version of Christianity, but *true* Christianity. True Christianity is found on a hard and narrow path, filled with self-denial that leads only one way—to a blood-stained cross.

If you never encounter persecution as a Christian, it's either because you are not living your faith, sharing your faith, or you are sharing a disarmed version of the gospel. The words Jesus spoke were so confrontational that the religious leaders of His time wanted Him dead and eventually got their wish. John the Baptist preached the truth and confronted King Herod about the sexual sin he was living in. It cost him his head. Paul was beaten and stoned on many occasions and eventually was beheaded. Peter was crucified upside down. The Apostles, many disciples, early church fathers, and many persecuted Christians throughout history, have been persecuted and killed for the sake of the gospel.

But Jesus promises in Matthew 5 that those who are persecuted for His name sake will have treasure in heaven. If we are truly convinced that Jesus is the King of all Kings and that heaven is being prepared for us by Him, then persecution will not undo us—it will embolden us. You can call it what you want and the seeker-friendly churches can call it what they want, but when we refuse to boldly proclaim the gospel, rebuke sin, preach sound doctrine, and stand for Christ no matter what the cost, we are cowards. When we water down, edit out, or disarm Scripture because we don't want to be rejected, we are not only denying His words, we are denying Christ Himself.

> For whosoever shall be ashamed of me and of my words, of him shall the Son of man be ashamed, when he shall come in his own glory, and in his Father's, and of the holy angels.
>
> Luke 9:26 (KJV)

If we are ashamed of any part of Christ, being a Christian, or of His Word, then He is ashamed of us. The reason we would do this is either we do not truly believe, or we fear the opinion of man more than the opinion of God. Being least may mean being marginalized within the church itself. Sometimes standing for righteousness in the face of an American church that is designed to suit the desires of men, rather than worshiping Almighty God, can bring persecution and condemnation on you.

The true Church has never been destroyed or corrupted by persecution. In fact, persecution always makes the church stronger. What weakens and corrupts the church is prosperity, political power, comfort, and complacency. The Scripture is clear that God's greatness is seen best in our weakness. Scripture says that God uses the foolish things and the weak things of the world to confound the wisdom of the wise.

When we go to church or listen to a minister preach, we should separate the speaker's delivery, the way they look, and their preaching style from what they preach. We should always be looking to see the message of Jesus and the true gospel, weighing every word on the scale of the Scripture. That is why we must study the Bible and the teachings of Jesus for ourselves so that we will not be deceived.

When we twist the teachings of Jesus to accommodate our message or our wants, we commit heresy of the highest order. Let us remember that we study Scripture to find and know God, not to find and know ourselves. There is no higher knowledge than the gospel and no greater pursuit in life than losing your life to be found in Christ.

As Christians, what is the greatest desire of our heart? Is it knowing God, bringing glory to His name, and drawing the world to Him? Are we consumed with eternity, or that hollowness of temporal things and worldly possessions? Those who truly humble themselves in this life for the sake of the kingdom will be lifted up in the future because they invested in eternity. That is Jesus. He is a treasure of incomparable riches whose glory will never cease to shine. The greatest joy of our existence will be to one day behold Him face to face. There is no greater crown to bear, or honor to behold, than to stand justified in God's presence because of Christ and to enjoy His presence forever. Those who partake in His suffering will also share in His glory.

> Now there is in store for me the crown of righteousness, which the Lord, the righteous Judge, will award to me on that day—and not only to me, but also to all who have longed for his appearing.
>
> 2 Timothy 4:8 (NIV)

CHAPTER 6

CULTURE OF SELF

But mark this: There will be terrible times in the last days. People will be lovers of themselves, lovers of money, boastful, proud, abusive, disobedient to their parents, ungrateful, unholy, without love, unforgiving, slanderous, without self-control, brutal, not lovers of the good, treacherous, rash, conceited, lovers of pleasure rather than lovers of God— having a form of godliness but denying its power. Have nothing to do with such people.

2 Timothy 3:1-5 (NIV)

Kingdom culture is that of the nature of God who was revealed in the person of Jesus Christ. Christ's nature is one of favoring others over oneself, serving not being served, humility, meekness, and mercy. God is love and full of grace; but God is also a God of justice. His judgments are always just and fair. He is also a God of wrath, but the Bible says that He is patient and slow to anger. God's majesty is unequaled, but so is His goodness and that fact alone reveals a great deal about His character.

Human nature on the other hand is completely different. Although we are created in the likeness and image of God, due to the fall of mankind there is not a part of us that is untainted and corrupted by sin. Humans don't chase status and wealth to be humble and meek, we chase status and wealth because we are hungry for power and control. Even though some do it with a false humility, the corruption of it is all the same.

God doesn't seek or chase power or greatness; it is not a pursuit or a position He seeks. Because He is good, He has chosen to manifest in meekness and humility in the teachings and person of Jesus Christ. But make no mistake, God is sovereign, all powerful, and above all things. God is good, not in the way we mean good, but with a goodness unparalleled and untainted by corruption. His goodness is not in response to our goodness, just like His love isn't increased by our love for Him, or diminished by our lack of love for Him. The Triune God is fully loving and utterly selfless.

One of the great distinctions between the person of Jesus, His teachings, and fallen and sinful human beings is that Jesus' nature is selfless. Jesus speaks in Matthew 5, 6, and 7 about what the life of a disciple should look like and what character attributes a Christian should have. He said things like "the meek shall inherit the earth," and "the first shall be last."

Under inspiration of the Holy Spirit, Paul outlines what a person outside of Christ's life will look like, or as he calls it "life in the flesh." Then he outlines what a person in Christ should look like, which he calls "walking in the Spirit." In Galatians 5, Paul lists what fruit the life of a believer should be producing and what the life of someone outside Christ naturally produces.

> So I say, walk by the Spirit, and you will not gratify the desires of the flesh. For the flesh desires what is contrary to the Spirit, and the Spirit what is contrary to the flesh. They are in conflict with each other, so that you are not to do whatever you want. But if you are led by the Spirit, you are not under the law.
>
> The acts of the flesh are obvious: sexual immorality, impurity and debauchery; idolatry and witchcraft; hatred, discord, jealousy, fits of rage, selfish ambition, dissensions, factions and envy; drunkenness, orgies, and the like. I warn you, as I did before, that those who live like this will not inherit the kingdom of God.
>
> But the fruit of the Spirit is love, joy, peace, forbearance, kindness, goodness, faithfulness, gentleness and self-control. Against such things there is no law. Those who belong to Christ Jesus have crucified the flesh with its passions and desires. Since we live by

the Spirit, let us keep in step with the Spirit. Let us not become conceited, provoking and envying each other.

Galatians 5:16-26 (NIV)

In 2 Timothy 3, it says that in the last days there will be terrible times. Are we in the last days? Biblically, the last days started after Jesus died, rose again, and ascended to heaven. But as we get closer to Christ's return, certain things will indicate we are drawing near to the end. The terrible times that the Apostle Paul writes about in 2 Timothy 3:1-5 are nothing new, but I believe as we get closer to the end these sinful attributes of man will be much more blatant and out in the open. This is definitely the case in America. We are living in a culture of self—self-empowerment, self-esteem, selfish ambition and self-love. The idea that people would be self-centered outside the church is one thing, but this culture of self is creeping into the church and is being embraced with open arms. It hasn't happened overnight, but elements of this new age, self-prompting philosophy are being widely accepted within the American church.

There is a great indication from the text that a self-centered theology will infiltrate the church and scores of people will adapt to a form of Christianity that is self-focused instead of Christ-focused. Let's be reasonable. God transforms our hearts when we surrender to Him, but He wants us to renew our minds through the Scripture. This is part of conforming to the image of Christ. We live in a culture that makes decisions based on how we feel rather than what is right or what is true. Always doing what feels right can lead us far away from living a life that pleases God. We must use our minds; but since our minds are stained by sin and are depraved according to God, how can we know what is right?

Therefore, I urge you, brothers and sisters, in view of God's mercy, to offer your bodies as a living sacrifice, holy and pleasing to God—this is your true and proper worship. Do not conform to the pattern of this world, but be transformed by the renewing of your mind. Then you will be able to test and approve what God's will is—his good, pleasing and perfect will.

Romans 12:1-2 (NIV)

Throughout Paul's epistles there is a recurring theme. First, he lays out sound doctrine and then he applies the practical application. Sound doctrine is truth according to the Scripture, so any practical application must be in light of that truth. When we make ourselves the focus, or try to be practical outside the fenced-in safety of sound doctrine, we are out of bounds. Renewing our minds through study of the Scripture helps us live lives that are pleasing to God. When we try to be practical without renewing our minds through the Scripture, what we end up with is something selfish, something based more on how we feel rather than Godly reason. We should never base decisions on our feelings and emotions. We need something that is sure and unchanging to guide us no matter how we feel. We must, as Christians, determine what is practical for our lives based on the sound doctrine found in the Scripture.

Christian doctrine has been infiltrated by self-help authors, motivational speakers, and life coaches who call themselves pastors. It would be better for them if they did not do this, because God will judge the preacher, pastor, and teacher more strictly. But without those titles, no one would buy their books and products. Some of these people are outright charlatans while others are as deceived as the people who buy their books. In either case, we will all give an account of whether or not we were faithful in our preaching and teaching of God's precious and sacred word.

Not many of you should become teachers, my fellow believers, because you know that we who teach will be judged more strictly.

James 3:1 (NIV)

As a pastor myself, these words weigh heavily on me. It is a huge responsibility to be a minister of the gospel, but much of the burden can be displaced if we are doing what we should be doing as pastors: proclaiming the Word of God, preaching the gospel, living above reproach, correcting, rebuking encouraging, and praying. This is the true call and life of a pastor.

It's interesting that in 2 Timothy 3, Paul names horrific characteristics that we would expect find outside the church, but gives an indication that it will be a problem inside the church. Lovers of money, lovers of themselves, proud, and lovers of pleasure. I am not a prophet, but it appears that in the American Evangelical church, those times are already here. Christian book stores, so-called Christian television, and Christian popular culture, is overrun with prosperity-centered books, Christian inspirational books, and teachings that teach a self-centered gospel, which is far from sound doctrine.

The message of self-esteem, self-love and self-empowerment are not compatible with the gospel of Jesus Christ. The Scripture doesn't tell us to empower ourselves; the Scripture calls us to deny ourselves. The seduction of a theology focused on self-improvement doesn't seem that bad at first glance, but if the true solution could be found in you then we wouldn't need God.

God is not another element we add to the portfolio of our life to give us a little more depth, or to help us be more successful. God is the sovereign creator of the universe and we are His creation. God owes us nothing, so we should be in awe that He sacrificed so much to have fellowship with us. This fellowship is available for those who realize that they stand guilty before God due to their sin, repent of their sin, and truly surrender their lives to Christ and follow Him.

THE PROBLEM OF PLEASURE

Many in our culture think that God owes them an explanation or believe that if they can somehow show that God is unfair or pretend He doesn't exist, that they are not subject to His authority. But if the God of the Bible truly does exist, then it doesn't matter if we accept it or reject it, we are still subject to His judgment.

If I committed a crime and was arrested for breaking the law and went to appear before the judge, I would be subject to his or her authority. I could say that they were unfair, or mean, or simply say that I didn't accept them as a judge, or pretend they weren't there. But when they give their ruling and announce my sentence, none of my reasonings would matter. Not accepting reality doesn't change reality, it usually just compounds the consequences when we finally have to face it.

Many people choose to pretend that God doesn't exist or they refuse to believe in a God who would allow pain and suffering in the world. In Christian apologetics this is what we call the problem of pain. C.S. Lewis wrote an excellent book about this topic titled *The Problem of Pain* and I highly recommend this book. In it he says, "We can ignore even pleasure. But pain insists upon being attended to. God whispers to us in our pleasures, speaks in our conscience, but shouts in our pains: it is his megaphone to rouse a deaf world." It's interesting that people who live in other parts of the world where there is much more pain and suffering seldom have this objection to Christianity. It's mostly in the West and especially in America. In fact, I believe this to be one of the major reasons Jesus taught that it was hard for the rich to enter heaven because the rich have the illusion that they are fine without God. It's only in the awareness of our desperate need for God that we surrender our lives to God. Self-sufficiency is a lie. Also, when we are blessed in this life and we realize that all blessing and provision comes from God, we will feel compelled to be a blessing. I say compelled because those who give with the illusion of self-sufficiency do so out of arrogance instead of gratefulness.

I believe the problem of pain and suffering to be such a strong objection to us in the West because we are such a self-centered society, saturated with pleasure. We think everything should be fair, fun, and entertaining, and when reality fails to live up to that impossible stipulation, we become depressed and discontent, and in some cases, even to the point of suicide.

Christian apologist Ravi Zacharias says, "This is a generation that listens with its eyes and thinks with its feelings." I couldn't agree more. Because of this, many preachers have begun to preach to people's *felt needs* rather than preaching the gospel. Feel good, self-centered messages may draw people in, but they will never transform them, change them, or sustain them. Only the truth found in the gospel and the person of Jesus Christ could ever do that.

The truth is what will set us free—not finding something we can live with, but finding something that we cannot live without, and encountering something that will transform us. We desire pleasurable stimulation so much that when something doesn't overload our senses, we call it depression. One of our greatest problems in the West is excess. It's funny how excess doesn't fill us up, but instead it makes us hungry for more: eating disorders, depression of every kind, drug addiction, sex addiction, shopaholics, workaholics . . . the list goes on and on. Most people in our country have more than enough to survive. People on every level of American society are in debt because we lead lifestyles of compulsion and excess. We will never find contentment in pleasure or materialism. True contentment is found only in a soul that has found peace with its Creator.

The empty and powerless version of the gospel preached today from many American pulpits is born out of our vain attempt to reconcile the gospel to the American dream. I love this country; I am thankful for all the blessings that being an American has afforded me. But just like Israel in the Old Testament, when we disconnect from God's righteousness and turn to idols and wicked living, we should expect God's wrath, not God's grace.

I pray for this country and its leaders; I pray that God has mercy on us. I pray that Christians will begin to fast and pray and turn back to Christ. But be sure of this: if we do not repent and turn from our sin, as a nation we will sit under God's judgment, just like any person who refuses to repent and turn from their sin.

A POWERLESS RELIGION

It's hard to not get caught up in the spirit of this age. If you want to live a life that is holy and pleasing to God you have to really work at separating yourself from a culture that is constantly lacerating your conscience while telling you not to worry and everything is all right. Deep down we know this is not true.

I'm not saying that people shouldn't give to others or have a social conscience. The message of social justice is popular today and it's hard because as a culture, we want to be thought of as caring, socially aware, and responsible people, but at a base level we are unwilling to do much at a personal cost to ourselves. We are willing to pay more for organic chicken raised on farms where they are not caged or mistreated because it is trendy. On the other hand, we are willing to murder a baby in the womb that might inconvenience our future, even though it was our reckless behavior that caused the unwanted pregnancy in the first place.

I'm not saying that all Christians agree with this. What I'm saying is that we have become so passive in the name of tolerance and comfort that we are unwilling to call out sin and call out evil. Much of this because we have a flawed view of the love of Jesus. God calls us to forgive sin when a person repents, not for us to tolerate it—especially in the church.

> "So watch yourselves. If your brother or sister sins against you, rebuke them; and if they repent, forgive them. Even if they sin against you seven times in a day and seven times come back to you saying 'I repent,' you must forgive them."
>
> Luke 17:3-4 (NIV)

We are told by many modern preachers, life coaches, and motivational speakers, that the problem is we don't value ourselves enough. What we need is more self-esteem and if we dig deep enough the solution is inside of us. Unfortunately, that is simply not true. We are not the solution; we are the problem. The problem isn't that we don't value ourselves enough, the problem is that we value ourselves above all else. The solution in all cases is to put God first and live in accordance to the Scriptures. This is the only way people who are selfish or self-deprecating, will live lives that honor God. The goal of our lives should ultimately be to honor God, not to find individual self-fulfillment, although leading a God-honoring life will lead to a life of fulfillment.

> . . . having a form of godliness but denying its power. Have nothing to do with such people.
>
> 2 Timothy 3:5 (NIV)

This self-centered version of Christianity that is full of pleasure seeking, selfish ambition, and arrogance may attract a crowd and may be popular, but in the words of Paul, it is powerless. Not only is it powerless, but it is poison to true believers. This is why Paul says in his letter to Timothy to stay away from such people. The Scripture says that God resists the proud, but gives grace to the humble. God resists pride, so can there be a selfish version of Christianity? I believe that pride, arrogance, and selfishness is a test to expose things that are false or corrupt in the faith. What is the power that they deny? The gospel! The true gospel of Jesus Christ. A gospel that is centered on self and personal gain is a false gospel and I believe it is the *other gospel* Paul refers to in Galatians 1:6-10. It is the opposite of everything Jesus taught and did, and of everything Paul taught and the way he lived.

These are not small errors. You have to intentionally distort or blindly overlook the main teachings of Jesus and the message of the gospel to come up with the gospel of prosperity, or a theology built around us rather than one focused on God. But it's easy to do if the climate is right, and post-modern America has the perfect environment for it.

I am astonished that you are so quickly deserting the one who called you to live in the grace of Christ and are turning to a different gospel— which is really no gospel at all. Evidently some people are throwing you into confusion and are trying to pervert the gospel of Christ. But even if we or an angel from heaven should preach a gospel other than the one we preached to you, let them be under God's curse! As we have already said, so now I say again: If anybody is preaching to you a gospel other than what you accepted, let them be under God's curse!

> Am I now trying to win the approval of human beings, or of God? Or am I trying to please people? If I were still trying to please people, I would not be a servant of Christ.
>
> Galatians 1:6-10 (NIV)

How is it that we have found a way to please both people and Christ and serve both money and God? Let's be honest, we haven't. Paul preached the true gospel of Christ and it didn't always please people. More often, it offended people because the true gospel is a call to repentance, and repentance for sin is the door that leads to salvation from sin through the power and forgiveness bought by our Savior Jesus Christ.

> For I am not ashamed of the gospel, because it is the power of God that brings salvation to everyone who believes: first to the Jew, then to the Gentile. For in the gospel the righteousness of God is revealed—a righteousness that is by faith from first to last, just as it is written: "The righteous will live by faith."
>
> Romans 1:16-17 (NIV)

The gospel is the power of Christianity. Like the Scripture says, it brings salvation to everyone who believes. Without the gospel, Christianity is nothing. It is powerless to change anything or anyone. This is why a social gospel is powerless. Doing good deeds is a good thing and Christians should feed the poor and take care of the sick, but don't think for a minute that this cancels out our sins. The gospel is the way a holy God chose to bring salvation to sinful mankind. A social gospel doesn't deal with sin. If we live a life of doing good deeds we will still die in our sins, because it's only through the repentance of sin and faith in Christ that we will escape God's just judgment.

We have bought into the lie that we are the center of the universe or the star of our own show. We do play a part, but in the body of Christ each part is important to the body. Who we are matters only when we are connected to Christ. Our society, and even much of the church, tells us that we should do what we feel, or follow our dreams. Or that it's God's will for us to rise to the top. The truth is you were made to fill a particular role in the body of Christ. It's not about personal greatness, or personal success, it's about being faithful in the place where God has placed you.

Alistair Begg, a preacher whom I respect at Cleveland's Parkside Church in Ohio, gave a great analogy of the body of Christ by using the illustration of a symphony orchestra. They are made up of many musicians, playing many different instruments, doing many different things, but because they are following the same music all that sound makes an amazing score that evokes feeling and emotion. It's beautiful and amazing because every musician plays their part, waits their turn, and what is produced could never be simulated by a soloist. Some parts may be noticed more than others, but a symphony isn't about a part—it's about the whole.

Christ is our conductor, arranger, and star of the show. Let us never forget this. Apart from Him we can do nothing. Christianity will never be about making Jesus a part of our life, but rather about making our entire life a part of Christ. He is the vine and the way, the truth and the life.

> Do not love the world or anything in the world. If anyone loves the world, love for the Father is not in them. For everything in the world—the lust of the flesh, the lust of the eyes, and the pride of life—comes not from the Father but from the world. The world and its desires pass away, but whoever does the will of God lives forever.
>
> 1 John 2:15-17 (NIV)

CHAPTER 7

NARROW ROAD CHRISTIANITY

We tend to seek the path of least resistance. The "easy way" so to speak. As Christians, we shouldn't look for the easy way *or* the hard way. We should be focused on walking down the path of truth no matter where it leads. We should be far more concerned about the *character* of our life than the *condition* of our life. But, because we have a fallen sin nature, unfortunately doing what's right is often a struggle, and when it comes to following Christ it is completely unnatural to us. This is why the Scripture says, regarding following Jesus, that we must deny ourselves.

In the Scriptures, Jesus frequently speaks about self-denial. He makes it clear that living by the status quo, and going with the flow, isn't what true Christianity looks like. This is not a popular message currently, and I'm sure it has never been a popular message in any age. Due to the rejection of absolute truth, the rise of secular atheism, and a culture that thinks it has outgrown God, we have an environment in which any personal discomfort for the sake of Christ is minimized or considered unnecessary altogether.

> "Enter through the narrow gate. For wide is the gate and broad is the road that leads to destruction, and many enter through it. But small is the gate and narrow the road that leads to life, and only a few find it."
>
> Matthew 7:13-14 (NIV)

Popular modern Christianity is broad; it minimizes sin, repentance, and sacrifice. Matthew 7:13-14 truly is a hard saying because our flesh is weak and wants it easy. You will be persecuted for preaching the full counsel of God. Everyone is born on the broad road because we are born into sin. But the path of the disciple of Jesus hinges on the teachings of Jesus; therefore, Jesus says, "Those who love me will obey my commands." You are not really a disciple of someone if you knowingly don't live by their teachings. To be a disciple means to discipline yourself to a certain way of life, prescribed by the teacher.

So many within the church take a pantheistic approach, which means they take the parts of Jesus' teachings they like and incorporate those into their lives, but leave behind the parts they don't like, or that don't fit into their lifestyle. The term *pantheism* means that there are many ways to God. To say that there are parts of the teachings of Jesus that are necessary and parts that are optional is pantheistic in nature.

To be called a disciple of someone's teachings, it implies that you carefully incorporate their philosophy and teachings into your life. Being a disciple of Jesus goes far beyond merely living by His teachings, though. It is inviting Him to take up residence in your life through His Spirit which transforms you. This is what it means to be born again. You are literally born anew in the Spirit to a brand-new life. Many preach that living as a disciple doesn't matter as much. I believe that the Scripture indicates that if you are transformed you will live according to His Word; perhaps not all at once, but definitely more and more every day. He not only commands us to live by His commands, but He empowers us to as well.

It's interesting to me that so many people who live so many ways claim to be in relationship with Jesus. I guess there are many ways to have a relationship with someone, but we should be more concerned with what Jesus expects from us and not what our flawed view tells us. Repeatedly in the Scripture, I see Jesus setting the terms of what kind of relationship He wishes to have with us. He wants our love, our obedience, and for us to be His disciples.

The apostle Paul calls himself a son by adoption, but more often he refers to himself as a servant of Christ or an apostle of Christ. If we are in Christ we are sons of God, but we should be careful not to let an American view of what sonship means distort our view and reverence of the God who chose us. We should consider ourselves sons who choose to be servants and disciples. If Jesus came to serve and Paul and Peter called themselves servants, then we are not above the example they set.

When I read Matthew 7 it shakes me up a bit. No, honestly, it shakes me up a lot. In Matthew 7:13-14 Jesus says that only a few will find what He calls the narrow road that leads to life, but many walk down the broad road that leads to destruction. Jesus, the author of salvation, the way, the truth and the life, God in the flesh, is giving us what appears to be direct warning which says that just because many people are walking down a particular path doesn't mean it is the right way. In fact, it seems He is saying that the broad way of the crowd is probably the wrong way.

What is strange to me is that people within much of the American church seem to care little about the Scriptures, and care little about ensuring they are preaching sound doctrine. People get turned off when you talk about sound doctrine and staying true to the Scriptures. Many modern preachers don't necessarily speak against the Scripture but seem to think that they have something more important to say beyond the Scripture. Even when what they say is in direct opposition of basic and fundamental truths of the faith, anyone who draws attention to this will quickly be silenced by being called judgmental or legalistic. Sadly, we gauge what is sound by what is successful. This is a poor way to gauge spiritual things. *By their fruit you will know them.*

Culturally, we have an unhealthy view of money and unfortunately so do many within the church. Many preachers focus on money and being what they call *blessed.* Really, they are just building a theology to accommodate their own greed. Preaching "I'm okay, you're okay" sermons. Turning the house of the Lord into a place of worldly systems, business, and entertainment. Then, in Matthew 7:21-23, it lays it all out: not only are the masses who go with the flow on the broad road headed for destruction, but also the false prophets who deceive us as they preach us towards destruction. Not everyone who thinks they have avoided this fate really has. There will be many who think that although they lived a life of compromise on the broad road, and avoided the narrow path of sacrifice and self-denial, they will still spend eternity with a Savior that they didn't care to know in this life. It is by grace that we are saved and our deeds cannot save us, but we are saved by faith—a faith that does have something to do with deeds. Actions don't save us but similar to a tree where the fruit shows what kind of tree it is, our actions bear witness to our faith. The kind of relationship Jesus expects is an intimate one, built on complete faith and trust in Him.

> "Not everyone who says to me, 'Lord, Lord,' will enter the kingdom of heaven, but only the one who does the will of my Father who is in heaven. Many will say to me on that day, 'Lord, Lord, did we not prophesy in your name and in your name drive out demons and in your name perform many miracles?' Then I will tell them plainly, 'I never knew you. Away from me, you evildoers!'"
> Matthew 7:21-23 (NIV)

The relationship that Jesus wants is an intimate one and a trusting one, like that of a bride to her husband and of a child to their parent. The words "Lord, Lord" are so frightening here because the people saying it fully expect to be received by the Lord, but the casual relationship they had with Him wasn't enough.

The thought of this is chilling to me. So many people who truly expect to be welcomed in with open arms by the Lord, to be part of His joy and His glory, will be turned away. Churches all across our country are filled with people who fit this description. But where are the preachers of repentance who preach the true gospel? Where are the prophets of warning watching the walls of the city? They have been put to death or at least silenced by the spirit of Jezebel.

Most people's relationship with Jesus is casual at best and according to Matthew 7, that may not be enough. We must start preaching the true gospel once again. We must preach the message of repentance once again. Charles Spurgeon said, "If people must go to hell let them go with bruises and scratches on their legs and arms from where we tried with everything we had to pull them towards the truth". Or at the least with the words of truth we preached ringing in their ears.

Finally, in Matthew 7:24-29, Jesus gives an analogy about two houses. It would seem both were built in the same area and were subject to the same environment because both houses experienced the same storm, intense rain, flooding, and powerful wind. Jesus gives no indication that the houses themselves were different in anyway. In context of the entire chapter of Matthew 7, Jesus gives this comparison of a house built on the rock and one that was built on the sand. They look the same and by all outward appearances are the same, until the storm comes.

This story should make us examine the foundation of what our life is truly built on. There is nothing more important than this. Is the surety of our salvation built on what the Bible says about following Jesus? Or is it built on what culture says, what our feelings tell us, or what we hope is true? I have had many disturbing conversations with people who overlook, minimize, and altogether ignore Scriptures of warning and direction based on something as trivial as their feelings. There is nothing more foolish than this. Putting our feelings above all else is truly what it means to build your house on the sand. Overlooking the words of the unchanging Savior, as written in Scripture, because they don't line up with what you feel is nothing less than rejecting Christ Himself. We can talk about our relationship with Christ all we want, we can say we did many things for the church, we can give money and time to great causes, but in the end all that will matter is whether or not everything in your life was built on a real and intimate relationship with the solid foundation Himself, Jesus Christ. No matter what makes up the materials of the "Christian style" house you build your life with, it's all meaningless if the foundation isn't sure and true. Without Christ your life will fall with a great crash and wash away.

Christ is the rock in the story and a life truly built on Christ will stay standing, not just in this life but in the life to come. People take so much of what Jesus said and try to apply it to whatever suits them. They like to say they are using the principles of Jesus and maybe sometimes they are, but this story isn't about anything other than what it plainly says. Those who hear what Jesus teaches and live it out are the ones who have a firm foundation that will endure everything, including death.

The one who lives life on the broad road and doesn't bear fruit and has a casual acquaintance with Jesus is building his or her house on the sand. Although it looks good in this life, one day when the storms and trials come, it will be shown for what is lacking—a true foundation. It will permanently crash down and be washed away.

> Anyone who falls on this stone will be broken to pieces; anyone
> on whom it falls will be crushed.
>
> Matthew 21:44 (NIV)

Jesus is the Rock, the Firm Foundation, and the Chief Cornerstone and whoever falls on Him will be broken and whoever He falls on will be crushed. Why? Because He is the truth. The truth can't change or be changed. It changes whatever it comes into contact with; it crushes untruth. Jesus is not only the Rock but His gospel is also the stumbling block by which men will either become broken through repentance or get broken by His justice.

> ... but we preach Christ crucified: a stumbling block to Jews and
> foolishness to Gentiles ...
>
> 1 Corinthians 1:23 (NIV)

Narrow-Path Christianity begins and ends with the gospel and with Christ; everything else is secondary. As we begin to follow Jesus and have true fellowship with Him, we first must accept Christ as Lord and as our only way of salvation. We must repent of our sins and start to live a life of discipleship as the Holy Spirit begins to conform us to the image of Christ through the Scriptures. Jesus is the only way to God and it's only through Him that we truly find salvation from our sins.

As disciples of Jesus, we should be students of the Scriptures, not for the sake of amassing and obtaining knowledge, but to discover the character of God and to learn how to live lives that please Him. A mere knowledge of God isn't enough though. If it were, Satan wouldn't have been cast out. And how about Judas? He probably knew the words of Jesus inside and out. He was in Jesus' inner circle for three and a half years but became disillusioned and betrayed Him. Why? Judas was following what He thought Jesus was, and who he hoped Jesus was, rather who He truly was. Once He saw that the actual purpose of Jesus didn't line up with what he wanted, he betrayed Him. We must come to Christ broken and to the Scriptures humbly, and to always be willing to let the Bible shape our lives, not our selfish desires.

If we say we accept Christ but reject His words, what are we actually doing? We are inventing a different version of Christ and in essence rejecting the true Savior. We are also misrepresenting Jesus, and this is a dangerous place to be. It's not hard as long as we are completely surrendered to knowing Christ and who He is and remembering that anything else we experience with God will always line up with the Scripture. If we are dedicated students of God's Word and are people of prayer, we will thrive and grow in Christ.

Remember when something in your heart or mind doesn't agree with the Scripture, what needs to change is in you, not the Scripture. If you have the Spirit of God living in you, that is the same Spirit that inspired the Bible so the two should always agree. If it seems that they don't, then perhaps you don't understand the Scripture. Or you're confusing what you *think* is the

Spirit with your feelings and your flesh. People who are true people of the Spirit are also people of God's Word, because it is the same thing. We need God's Word to cut through what we think is true and what is actually true. This is discipleship.

> For the word of God is quick, and powerful, and sharper than any two-edged sword, piercing even to the dividing asunder of soul and spirit, and of the joints and marrow, and is a discerner of the thoughts and intents of the heart.
>
> Hebrews 4:12 (KJV)

Our hearts and desires can deceive us, but the never-changing Word of God will always cut through the wants of the soul to the need of the Spirit, because it is Christ Himself. Don't we realize that Christ Himself is the Word? John explains this to us in the first lines of his gospel, when he pens some of the deepest words in the Scripture.

> In the beginning was the Word, and the Word was with God, and the Word was God. He was with God in the beginning. Through him all things were made; without him nothing was made that has been made. In him was life, and the life was the light of all mankind. And the light shines in the darkness, and the darkness has not overcome it.
>
> John 1:1-5 (NIV)

Jesus is the key to everything, the answer to every mystery, and the fulfillment of every tenant of our faith. The reason why the road is so narrow in true Christianity is because it is found only in the person of Jesus Christ. The fulfillment of the Old Testament is found only in Christ. Our only way to salvation is found in Christ. The only hope for humanity is found in Christ. The answer to every question is somehow found in Christ. He is the answer to all things because He is the origin of all the things. This what John is saying in John 1:1-5. Christ, who is the Word, became flesh and fulfilled all things and made a way of salvation for us. That very word is revealed to us in the

Scriptures so when one discounts the value of God's written word, it is to discount God Himself.

We are all born on the broad road of life, in sin and headed for destruction. Jesus is the straight gate with the small entrance that leads to life. He made the way, and also sent His Spirit for us. Throughout the ages people have told themselves that they can stay on the broad road and still somehow avoid destruction, but it simply isn't true. It's only through Christ as revealed in His Word that we will be saved and have life and have it more abundantly.

> "Jesus answered, 'I am the way and the truth and the life. No one comes to the Father except through me.'"
>
> John 14:6 (NIV)

CHAPTER 8

THE NICEST WOLVES
I KNOW

Watch out for false prophets. They come to you in sheep's clothing, but inwardly they are ferocious wolves. By their fruit you will
recognize them. Do people pick grapes from thorn bushes, or figs
from thistles? Likewise, every good tree bears good fruit, but a
bad tree bears bad fruit. A good tree cannot bear bad fruit, and
a bad tree cannot bear good fruit. Every tree that does not bear
good fruit is cut down and thrown into the fire. Thus, by their
fruit you will recognize them.

Matthew 7:15-20 (NIV)

Jesus tells us to watch out for false prophets who are dressed in sheep's
clothing but inwardly they are ferocious wolves. For some reason no matter
how unbiblical a preacher's teachings are in the American church today, it
is rare for anyone to be disturbed enough to speak a word of rebuke. The
standard for sound doctrine is low in this day and age. We are so terrified
to be labelled judgmental or legalistic that we will endure nearly any sort of
error. I am talking about heresy that is so prevalent and so unbiblical that any
Bible-believing Christian should refute it, but in the American church apparently no heresy is bad enough to call out. In fact, the only sin in much of the
American church today is *calling sin a sin*. That is unacceptable.

The Bible is no longer the standard for what is right and what is true in much of our church culture today. It is strange that even when you quote the words of Jesus directly, you are still in danger of being perceived as judgmental by other Christians. The sad reality is that anything said that doesn't make us happy is called judgmental. The ironic part is that most of these hard teachings spoken by Jesus are intended to help us avoid judgment. This view, this mindset, has opened the door to ferocious wolves who come in and abuse the flock. As we have drifted from true Christian discipleship and being true students of the Bible, we have opened the door to every kind of false teacher and false teaching under the sun.

I knew we were in deep trouble when a few years ago the pastor of one of the largest churches in America refused to state that Jesus is the only way to God. This happened in front of millions of television viewers. He simply stated that it wasn't his place to say yes or no on the subject.

Larry King with CNN restated his question several times to ensure that the pastor understood what he meant. This pastor held his ground and refused to state that Jesus is the only way by which we are saved and that all things outside of Christ are subject to judgment.

Larry King then asked him, will Mormons go to heaven, will Buddhists go to heaven, will atheists go to heaven? The pastor's response was that he would not judge anyone. King wasn't asking him to judge anyone, he merely wanted to know if he believed in the biblical view of salvation through Jesus Christ alone. What an amazing opportunity this pastor had at that moment to present the gospel, but for some reason he did not.

I am not surprised that a prosperity-driven televangelist would refuse to say emphatically that Jesus was the only way to God, because a person in his position doesn't want to divide his audience. This pastor doesn't want to upset anyone. He must remain as *middle-of-the road* as possible to keep his viewers happy. They will then continue watching his television show and buying his books.

This is heresy. If you refuse to speak the truth about Jesus because you don't want men to think you are judgmental, you are a coward and far from faith. What did surprise me, however, was the lack of outrage and rebuke from the mainstream of Christianity. Not only did very few call this out, but the few who did were called judgmental and harsh.

Many people I talk to give responses such as, *His messages are so encouraging,* or *He's so nice and friendly how could you say anything negative about him?* The truth is this pastor does seem nice and friendly. When he talks it comes across in a passive sort of *aw-shucks* way—always smiling and sweet. The problem is that niceness doesn't matter one bit when talking about biblical truth and sound doctrine. Jesus said if you are ashamed of me before men I will be ashamed of you before my Father (Mark 8:38). Trust me, that is a place none of us want to be.

What part of *wolf in sheep's clothing* do we not understand? A false teacher isn't going to come out looking evil and openly cursing Jesus. He is going to be a nice, likable guy. His outward appearance and demeanor will be appealing, but his message will be false and lead to destruction. We must realize that the one big reason we are susceptible to false teachers is a lack of sound doctrine. I have heard people say within charismatic circles that they would rather be Spirit-led than doctrinally sound. That is a total contradiction to think that you can be Spirit-led without being doctrinally sound. The Bible was inspired by the Spirit and has everything we need for a life of Godliness. If the Spirit of God leads us, you can be sure it will line up with the Scripture and will not contradict it.

> But there were also false prophets among the people, just as there will be false teachers among you. They will secretly introduce destructive heresies, even denying the sovereign Lord who bought them—bringing swift destruction on themselves. Many will follow their depraved conduct and will bring the way of truth into disrepute. In their greed these teachers will exploit you with

fabricated stories. Their condemnation has long been hanging over them, and their destruction has not been sleeping.

2 Peter 2:1-3 (NIV)

The Scripture here doesn't tell us to watch out for false teachers outside the church, it says to watch out for false teachers that will come from among us. This text is saying that from inside the church there will be preachers, prophets, and teachers that secretly introduce heresies and even deny the sovereign Lord who bought them. Here in America we have every variety of religion to choose from and even within true Christianity there are many kinds of churches and denominations. So how do we sort it all out? We let the Bible do that. We weigh everything on the scale of Scripture.

If human hands are involved in the church there will be imperfections, but that is okay. Imperfection doesn't necessarily mean that it is not sound or able to be used. We don't discard things because they are imperfect or have some minor imperfections. We discard things that are *not sound*, like a jug that doesn't hold water or a guitar with a warped neck. The soundness of Christianity doesn't center around the people who are part of it; it is centered around the Scriptures and the person of Christ. This is what makes the Scripture so important. It truly reveals the person of Christ and contains everything we need for life and Godliness. When we have disagreements or misunderstandings as the body of Christ we have something to appeal to. If we are true students of the Scripture and focus on the person of Jesus Christ and the gospel, as revealed in Him and fulfilled through Him, we are off to a great start.

We may not agree on the meaning of every minor detail in the Bible, but if we agree on the essentials and humbly approach the Scripture as the authoritative answer for everything in our lives, we will be headed in the right direction. We take the narrow path aimed at conforming to the image of Christ as we follow closely after Him. We are imperfect students of a perfect

Scripture revealed to us through our perfect Savior. True Christianity is centered on Christ as revealed in the Scripture. Our path of discipleship is to become like Him and draw others toward Him. If we are not doing this, then we are headed in the wrong direction. When we teach things that change who Christ is in order to draw people toward Him, then we are actually drawing them *a different way*. Whether this is done intentionally or unintentionally, it is a false gospel.

IT IS WRITTEN

Be cautious of preachers and teachers who preach only topical messages, and who rarely reference the Bible. These preachers use the Scriptures as a nice garnish for the meal of wit and well-stated personal opinions that they serve up on various topics. Be very afraid of preachers who do not encourage you to read the Bible for yourselves and test the messages they deliver. Develop in yourself a strong biblical hermeneutic so that you get used to reading the Bible in light of its historical and contextual backdrop. There is no need to have a critical spirit when we listen to preaching, but rather have a humble, yet discerning, spirit. Realize that if you are in Christ, the same spirit that lives in you lives in the preacher. That is, of course, if he truly is in Christ himself. We cannot assume just because someone calls themselves a teacher or a pastor that what they are saying is sound. Everything should be filtered through the Scriptures and through prayer. A true pastor will want you to be a student of Scripture. We should never underestimate the power of the Scriptures. The use of Scripture is how Jesus overcame the temptation of Satan in the desert:

> Then Jesus was led by the Spirit into the wilderness to be tempted by the devil. After fasting forty days and forty nights, he was hungry. The tempter came to him and said, "If you are the Son of God, tell these stones to become bread."
>
> Jesus answered, "It is written: 'Man shall not live on bread alone, but on every word that comes from the mouth of God.'"

Then the devil took him to the holy city and had him stand on the highest point of the temple. "If you are the Son of God," he said, "throw yourself down. For it is written: "'He will command his angels concerning you, and they will lift you up in their hands, so that you will not strike your foot against a stone.'"

Jesus answered him, "It is also written: 'Do not put the Lord your God to the test.'" Again, the devil took him to a very high mountain and showed him all the kingdoms of the world and their splendor. "All this I will give you," he said, "if you will bow down and worship me." Jesus said to him, "Away from me, Satan! For it is written: 'Worship the Lord your God and serve him only.'" Then the devil left him, and angels came and attended him.

Matthew 4:1-11 (NIV)

If relying on Scripture as his defense for temptation was good enough for Jesus, it should be good enough for us. Jesus continually quoted from the Scriptures. Jesus was the perfect example as well as God incarnate, so it is foolish to think we are beyond or above Him in anyway. False teachers reject the Bible in many ways. Some are more subtle than others, but anytime a preacher is less than reverent of the Scriptures, run away from them far and fast.

Some will use a verse as bait to lead off their messages as a hook so you will buy whatever lies they are telling you. However, the Scripture isn't the true focus of their message. It is strategically placed in an attempt to give their sermon credibility. Remember Satan did this also when trying to tempt Jesus.

Some will downplay the importance of Scripture and use it as a backdrop for their message which will have no true contextual connection to the sermon. We must remember that most false teachers will not be obvious. They will fit the mold and play the part of a pastor, but their messages will be focused more on self than on God. When we see God for who He is, and ourselves in light of that revelation, we should be utterly humbled. If we are not, we are deceived. It is impossible to view God in His rightful place and not realize how small we are by comparison. False teachers make easy work of people who don't truly know God and who are not dedicated to knowing Him through the Scriptures. If they can get someone to take their focus off of God and put it on themselves they are easy to deceive.

It's easy to preach to felt needs. It's easy to manipulate the Scriptures to seem that self-fulfillment is noble. Our sinful nature is susceptible to that. We want everything to be about us and we love it when a preacher gets up and tells us that seeking self-worth is good, that selfish ambition is noble, and that God is fine with our sinful desires. It is the disease of sin that causes us to turn our worship inward instead of upward. There is no such thing as self-fulfillment. The only true satisfaction in this life is to lose our life in Christ, and as the Apostle Paul says, to be found in Christ not having a righteousness of our own as based on the law, but one that comes through Christ on the basis of faith.

A false teacher relies on his own creativity and on stories and series that are worldly and appeal to the flesh instead of doing what a pastor, preacher, and teacher should do—proclaim the Scriptures to the best of their ability through the power of the Holy Spirit.

False teachers and preachers also tend to subtly minimize the glory and power of Jesus and emphasize their own power and influence. No false teacher comes out and denies Jesus; it is usually more about subtly moving away from the centrality of Christ. There is a popular celebrity preacher talking about moving away from saying things like "the Bible says" or "it is written" because he says that those phrases are not relevant anymore. His logic is this: *who cares if you're speaking the truth if nobody is listening.* This is poor logic and is born out of the flesh not the Spirit. Telling people what they want to hear because they don't want the truth isn't valid. This is like saying if the damned don't listen to you, damn yourself so they will. Calling into question the authority of the living Word of God might make you seem relevant and edgy, but putting your own words or wisdom on par with Scripture is beyond foolish. It is wicked. Our job is to proclaim the name of Jesus and the truth about Jesus as revealed in His Word no matter what. In fact, when people aren't listening and have fallen away, that is when truth matters more than ever.

> In the presence of God and of Christ Jesus, who will judge the living and the dead, and in view of his appearing and his kingdom, I give you this charge: Preach the word; be prepared in season and out of season; correct, rebuke and encourage—with great patience and careful instruction. For the time will come when people will not put up with sound doctrine. Instead, to suit their own desires, they will gather around them a great number of teachers to say what their itching ears want to hear. They will turn their ears away from the truth and turn aside to myths. But you, keep your head in all situations, endure hardship, do the work of an evangelist, discharge all the duties of your ministry.
>
> 2 Timothy 4:1-5 (NIV)

In 2 Timothy, the Apostle Paul writes to his son in the faith with a bold declaration. He says in the presence of Christ Jesus who will judge him and everyone else one day, Timothy, *I give you this charge: preach the word.* Not to be sensitive to the culture, or to make sure you are relevant in order to grow your church. The admonition was quite simply, *preach the word.* He tells him to do so in season and out of season, if it is fashionable or if it is not, if it easy or if it is not, if it is well received or if it is not. We must preach the full counsel of God according to the Scripture. And for people who call themselves Christian disciples, we as pastors must use God's Word to correct, rebuke, and encourage. I hear a lot of pastors talking about encouragement, but it's not very often that I hear a pastor, especially prosperity and word-faith pastors, talk about correction or rebuke.

If I were a little league baseball coach and one of my players was having trouble hitting the ball because their batting stance was wrong, I wouldn't encourage them to keep trying just so I wouldn't offend them or hurt their feelings. That would be insane. If I'm the coach, it's my job to help my player grow and be successful as a player.

First, I would stop them and correct their bad stance and bad hitting form. Then I would show them the correct way to stand and the right way to swing. If they reverted back to their old hitting habits I would rebuke them, but once they had their stance right and their swing was right I would encourage them.

Hit or miss I would keep encouraging them until they hit the ball. Encouraging people in sin that leads to destruction and calling it love is not only wrong, it's satanic. But it is two-sided, because false teachers are merely a product of the people who refuse the truth. The Scripture says that there will come a time when people will not endure sound doctrine, because it is not what they want to hear. They surround themselves with teachers who are false and are willing to preach a gospel that accommodates the greed in their heart, or their compromised lifestyle. It's a message that preaches a personal savior who will conform to your image instead of you conforming to His.

> This is what the Lord Almighty says: "Do not listen to what the prophets are prophesying to you; they fill you with false hopes. They speak visions from their own minds, not from the mouth of the Lord."
>
> Jeremiah 23:16 (NIV)

We need to be careful about telling people *the Lord says*, or *God told me to tell you this.* Sometimes hope is false hope and sometimes encouragement is not Godly. Many pastors tend to think any encouragement is good and that giving hope is also the right thing to do. But if we are encouraging people who are in sin and estranged from God, or telling unsaved people that there is hope found anywhere outside of Christ, we are preaching falsehood and maybe at the expense of someone's soul.

BEWARE OF FALSE PROPHETS

In Matthew 7:15 it says, "beware of false prophets." In the King James Version and in the New International Version it says, "watch out for false prophets." The fact that Jesus uses language like *beware* or *watch out* should grab our attention so that we meditate on the importance of these words.

Having an unbalanced, false Christian would be bad enough, but when they are a leader, teacher, or pastor, Jesus considered this dangerous enough to compare them to a ravenous wolf. We, then, should take notice.

> Dear friends, do not believe every spirit, but test the spirits to see whether they are from God, because many false prophets have gone out into the world.
>
> 1 John 4:1 (NIV)

Now obviously anyone who comes out and openly denies the incarnation of Christ is a false prophet. Jesus said to watch out because they will be crafty and cunning; therefore, we must test the spirits. Test their spirit by the Holy Spirit and the Scripture. False prophets are often great, charismatic speakers with the ability to hold people's attention, but being a great speaker doesn't mean that you are preaching the truth. False teachers will often twist the Scripture to accommodate their point, or to make their message sound interesting or compelling. Twisting the Scripture is the definition of a false teacher. The American church is full of charismatic preachers who are great speakers but poor expositors of the Scripture, and yet proclaiming the Scripture is what we have been called to do.

THE LOVE OF MONEY

One of the greatest indicators of a false teacher is the love of money. Money isn't evil and living in poverty doesn't make you holy, but greed and the love of money is a light into the heart of a man who is corrupt. Some pastors are so bold and arrogant that they unashamedly say that the gospel leads to worldly wealth. But even those who are too crafty to come right out and say it are exposed by their actions and by the opulent and shameful ways that they live. These men preach a message of worldly success in place of the gospel because this is what is in their hearts. Some are blatant and completely heretical, while others have let this creep into their church but haven't been consumed by it.

For an overseer, as God's steward, must be above reproach. He
must not be arrogant or quick-tempered or a drunkard or violent
or greedy for gain . . .

Titus 1:7

The reason why many in the church accept this heresy of worldly gain
instead of rebuking it is because deep down, they are also greedy for gain.
Repeatedly in the New Testament we are told to beware of the pitfalls that
come with money and that pastors shouldn't use the gospel for a means
to achieve financial gain. The American culture is one that admires greed
and measures success by the size of your house, the kind of car you drive,
and the amount of money you have in the bank. In our culture, there is no
shortage of men who write books, have websites, and advertise on television their personal systems and programs that will help you achieve success
and wealth.

Unfortunately, greed is not outside of the church only. False teachers and
charlatans have always been around and will always be until Christ returns.
With the rise of televangelism, celebrity preachers, and cult of personality-
style Christianity, the door has been opened to every kind of false teacher.
We are not only a society of greed, but we also worship at the altar of celebrity and much of Christianity is no different. Some celebrity preachers freely
promote non-biblical concepts and loosely say questionable things that fifty
years ago would have been called heresy by mainstream Christianity. Now
due to our worship of celebrity, we will discount nearly anything said by a
preacher who is famous. Many preachers look like rock stars of high fashion
and have immersed themselves so deeply into worldly culture you wouldn't
be able to separate them from any other worldly celebrity, either by their
words or their deeds.

What about living far above reproach or maintaining a humble lifestyle that honors God? There are too many different kinds of false teachers to try and lump them all in together, but this much is clear: any time

preachers twist Scripture to accommodate his teaching or lifestyle, anytime a message is preached that is not compatible with Scripture, or anytime preachers undermine the words of Jesus as revealed in the Scriptures, he reveals false teaching. Many times, we refuse to call someone a false teacher because we try to discern their intentions rather than what they teach. However, just because they might be deceived as well doesn't make them any less of a false teacher.

Jesus told us to watch out for them, to beware of them so in obedience to Him, so we should do exactly that. Using marketing to sell Jesus as a means to success is anti-biblical and in contrast to the teaching of the Scripture. Not all pastors in America have fallen into this trap; I wouldn't even say that most have. The presence of those who have fallen into this trap cast such a large shadow over the church, it's sometimes difficult to see beyond it. It is a real temptation for every pastor to fall into this. That is why we must be people of the Scripture and keep our eyes fixed firmly on Jesus.

Let's be clear. I am not saying money is good or bad. It depends on the place it has in your life. I am saying that pastors and preachers have a special responsibility to live far above reproach and distance themselves from the pursuit, or even the appearance of the pursuit, of riches. Using giving to the church and tithing as a scheme to teach people if they give they will achieve financial gain is manipulation to say the least. Anyone who gives to receive has already shown that their hearts are misguided. If you are giving to be rewarded, you have already received your reward. Tithe because God commands you to, not because you think that tithing will make you rich or bless you with financial increase.

> "No one can serve two masters. Either you will hate the one and love the other, or you will be devoted to the one and despise the other. You cannot serve both God and money."
>
> Luke 16:13 (NIV)

Greed is the largest gate that welcomes wolves into the sheep pen. And not just the greed of the false teacher or preacher, but the greed of the people who desire to hear that gain is godliness. You cannot serve both God and money. Think of a famous preacher who always preaches about financial gain as blessing and makes excuses for their opulence and lavish lifestyles, their mansions, sports cars, and lives of luxury and compare them to the words of the Apostle Paul in the book of 1 Timothy.

> If anyone teaches otherwise and does not agree to the sound instruction of our Lord Jesus Christ and to godly teaching, they are conceited and understand nothing. They have an unhealthy interest in controversies and quarrels about words that result in envy, strife, malicious talk, evil suspicions and constant friction between people of corrupt mind, who have been robbed of the truth and who think that godliness is a means to financial gain.
>
> But godliness with contentment is great gain. For we brought nothing into the world, and we can take nothing out of it. But if we have food and clothing, we will be content with that. Those who want to get rich fall into temptation and a trap and into many foolish and harmful desires that plunge people into ruin and destruction. For the love of money is a root of all kinds of evil. Some people, eager for money, have wandered from the faith and pierced themselves with many griefs.
>
> 1 Timothy 6:3-10 (NIV)

Paul says that godliness *with contentment* is great gain and that we should be content with food and the clothes on our backs. He also says that people who think that godliness is gain have been robbed of the truth. Paul says in this Scripture that anyone who teaches otherwise does not agree with the sound instruction of the Lord Jesus because they are conceited and understand nothing.

The love of celebrity, power, and influence just exposes a heart of greed. False teachers have this heart, but so do the people who sit under them clamoring to be comforted in their compromise and affirmed in their own greed.

KNOWING THE TRUTH

When U.S. Secret Service agents are trained to spot fake money, they don't train by looking at counterfeit bills, they train by studying real money. Why? Because if they know every detail of the genuine article they can easily spot anything that is out of place when they come across counterfeit bills. We can know what is false and what is true if we are serious students of the Scripture. We must base what is sound and what is not on the Scripture and the words of Jesus and call out teachers that contradict just like John the Baptist did, just like Jesus did, and just like the apostle Paul did.

The wolves that come to feed on the flock will sound good, look good, and be easy on the ear. We must be vigilant and on guard so that we are not also deceived. There is no time for complacency; we must live our lives intently on honoring God according to His Word, otherwise we are just wasting our lives. The road to hell is broad, easy, and paved with good intentions, but the road that leads to life is narrow and only a few will find it.

CHAPTER 9

THE YOKE OF SIN

Some people might get defensive of this biblical critique and the idea of questioning whether we can truly reconcile the gospel and Christian discipleship to the American dream, the American church, and our culture. But rest assured that I am not bashing America or the American church by any means. I am asking important questions about the condition we find ourselves in because I want God's blessing and favor to rest on our land. That is impossible if we are an unrepentant nation who loves sin.

As the church, we often get caught up in the issues that are a by-product of problems and trouble in our culture, rather than aiming at the root from which all these problems grow. America shares the same problem as the rest of the world in this time and in all times before us: we are under a yoke that is heavy. Although some have the illusion of being born free from it, no one really is. It is the yoke of sin.

We have false ideas about social issues and trouble. We think if we can feed the hungry and help the less fortunate that we will somehow prove to the world that the church and God are good, and then people will surrender to God. But we ignore the fact that the world loves darkness and good deeds can never undo that. Even if we somehow fixed every external problem in the world, we would still have the internal problem of the sinful heart of man (which is the cause of all the external problems anyway).

Few preachers preach about sin these days because they think that it is not encouraging. They would rather focus on the good things of Christianity. The truth is, until we honestly deal with sin there are no good things for us. Salvation is available only on the other side of repentance and repentance comes only with acknowledging our sins and surrendering our life to Christ. The church is full of unconverted, false Christians because they have never acknowledged and repented of their sin. If we didn't need forgiveness for our sins Jesus wouldn't have had to die for them.

It is because of this we get perhaps the hardest teaching of Jesus and that is the *exclusivity of Christ*. If we preach a message that doesn't call for the cross and a message that does not acknowledge our sin, it is rejecting the value of the cross. It implies that maybe sin wasn't a big enough issue to separate us eternally from God.

People who discount sin or avoid the topic altogether not only undermine the importance of the gospel, but also undermine the beauty and power of the gospel. The importance is obviously this: Jesus and what He accomplished on the cross is the most important part of Christianity. We must be very protective of the gospel. Without all the elements of the birth, life, death, and resurrection of Christ as revealed in the Scripture, Christianity is nothing more than a long-winded movement or social experiment. Without the all-encompassing burden and death sentence of sin set into motion at the fall of mankind in Genesis, the events of the entire the Old Testament would not have had to pave the way for the coming Savior. When we preach a message that says Jesus came to make your life better and take you to the next level in your business, your marriage, or whatever felt-need you wish to insert, we are completely misleading people. Jesus came to pay a debt that rightfully belonged to humanity because of sin. He didn't come to make our life better, He came to *give us life*.

> As for you, you were dead in your transgressions and sins, in which you used to live when you followed the ways of this world

and of the ruler of the kingdom of the air, the spirit who is now
at work in those who are disobedient. All of us also lived among
them at one time, gratifying the cravings of our flesh and following its desires and thoughts. Like the rest, we were by nature deserving of wrath.

Ephesians 2:1-3 (NIV)

We were dead in our transgressions and sin and deserved wrath by nature. We have all committed transgressions or evil acts because of our sin.
But sin isn't necessarily an act: it is the nature we were born with. This is
why we must deny, lay down, and put to death our old nature and take on a
new nature. This is the nature which we are born into when we surrender to
Christ. The importance of the gospel is that without it we would die in our
sins and forever be separated from God. A gospel without repentance from
sin disarms the power of the gospel.

> Now therefore mend your ways and your deeds, and obey the
> voice of the Lord your God, and the Lord will relent of the disaster
> that he has pronounced against you.

Jeremiah 26:13

The landscape of the United States has changed a great deal over the last
fifty years. Although many things have contributed to this cultural shift, one
thing is clear: we are for the most part now a post-Christian nation. We can
argue about what that actually means and what defines a Christian nation or
the differences between people who claim Christ and those who actually live
for Him, but once we removed God from our schools and public squares and
legalized abortion—which is simply the wholesale murder of babies in the
womb for the sake of convenience—we proved that we are not one nation
under God.

I spend a lot of my time traveling and preaching at different churches and
know that there are a lot of great churches, pastors, and men and women of

God all across this country. Jesus said He would build His church and the gates of hell would not prevail against it. But I can't help noticing the correlation between the systematic attack on Christianity in our country and the decline of morality, stability, law and order, and at the same time an increase of calamity of all kinds. We are quick to try to remove God from this equation because of poor theology and a misunderstanding of God's sovereignty. We say that God has nothing to do with any bad things that come upon us as a nation, but the Scriptures indicate that this is not outside the scope of possibility.

> Now the end is upon you, and I will send my anger upon you; I will judge you according to your ways, and I will punish you for all your abominations.
>
> Ezekiel 7:3

If God was willing to send calamity on Israel, the nation that He calls the apple of His eye, then why would we think America is any different? I don't claim to know the mind of God, nor would I be foolish enough to point fingers at people and say that I know what brings each trial or trouble. I am but a simple and weak servant of Christ, but the argument that God wouldn't do that or that He doesn't send judgment on the wicked is easily refuted in the Old Testament and the New Testament.

> The lot is cast into the lap, but its every decision is from the Lord.
>
> Proverbs 16:33 (NIV)

> I form the light and create darkness, I bring prosperity and create disaster; I, the Lord, do all these things.
>
> Isaiah 45:7 (NIV)

God sent forth His righteous judgment on many nations throughout history, including Israel after Christ ascended. When nations do evil in the sight of God they will sit under His judgment. God will also restrain His righteous judgment out of mercy hoping for repentance. God's goodness is not in question because He punishes the evil and the sinful. We are an evil and debauched nation. We are murderous, we are perverse and perverted, we endure every kind of evil, we are full of greed, idolatry, and blasphemy. We worship the idol of materialism, we tolerate every kind of sexual immorality, and we love violence. If you think I'm being harsh turn on your television, check in on social media, or listen to a secular radio station. We are subjected to so much junk that we have gotten used to the wholesale sin of our culture and nation.

The beauty in being honest about the condition we are in as a nation and as a church is that it's only by the truth that we will be set free. I am the pastor and program director of Sonrise Adult & Teen Challenge in Cache, Oklahoma, and deal with men who are coming out of addiction. I also was set free by Christ from the bondage of addiction and one thing that is clear is to me is this: until we are ready to face the truth there is no moving forward. This is not only true with addiction but in every part of life. Ignoring or denying a problem will never resolve it since it usually causes it to grow. Every sin is the same no matter how many times you pluck the fruit off the tree, it will always grow back and all the while the roots are growing stronger. The truth exposes the root. Digging up a developed root system is sometimes a long and hard process, but in the end, we need to completely dig up every area of our life that is in bondage to sin. The same goes for our country, and the same goes for the church.

Jesus doesn't merely know the truth or, like Solomon, have a mind full of wisdom about the truth; He *is* truth and the reflection of that truth is revealed to us in His living Word.

> Every good gift and every perfect gift is from above, and cometh down from the Father of lights, with whom is no variableness, neither shadow of turning.
>
> James 1:17 (KJV)

The remedy for sin is found in surrender and salvation through Jesus Christ. He has never wavered, faltered, missed the mark, fallen short, or changed. When God set His plan in motion to conquer sin and render death powerless, no part has ever been hindered or not come to pass. When God speaks, His subservient universe agrees. The fact that we don't understand many mysteries of the universe, the fall of man, or the deep and timeless workings of a sovereign and eternal God doesn't disprove Him, it confirms Him all the more. We are mere created beings that God gave the privilege to not only exist, but also the ability to know Him and commune with Him. If we think we have the right to make demands on the Creator or call Him to explain Himself or His actions to us, we are beyond deluded and live outside the scope of logic and reality.

The self-absorbed notion that God should somehow explain Himself or prove His fairness to His creation isn't an idea that was born in our time or in our culture. However, our modern American culture is an environment that fosters and promotes such a concept. Much like Israel in the Old Testament, we are a nation uniquely blessed by God, but now has rejected Him and turned to sin and idol worship and now we find ourselves at the precipice of judgment. America has let sin overtake us and much of the American church has become too comfortable and complacent to stand up for truth. We are too busy seeking prosperity and focusing on ourselves to see that sin isn't just crouching at our door, it has taken up residence in our house. Many pastors are too cowardly to confront sin because they are afraid that it might cost them something to stand up for the truth. Although there are many excuses and reasons for this, the truth is that we need pastors to preach the word and stand for truth and let the pieces fall where they may. We will give account for what we preach and what we refused to preach because we feared men more than we feared the Lord.

MODERN BAAL WORSHIP

In the Old Testament, Israel was rebuked repeatedly because of the worship of Baal. Baal was a god worshipped in many ancient Middle Eastern communities. The Canaanites considered him a fertility deity and one of the most important gods in the pantheon. He was also called the Lord of Rain and Dew, the two forms of moisture that were indispensable for fertile soil in Canaan. Although Israel was a nation who followed the Lord, it is apparent at certain times throughout the history of Israel they would forsake the worship of the Lord for the worship of Baal, or would attempt to blend the two. They would become complacent and begin to make compromises and let sin corrupt them little by little. Finally, God would send a prophet of warning who would call the nation to repentance. As history tells us, when they repented God would have mercy on them, but more often than not they would refuse and God would bring judgment on them. In some cases this meant hardship, slavery, exile, and the destruction of their land.

The message of the prophet isn't usually well received especially when the prophet comes into an evil situation and calls for people who are comfortable in compromise to repent and turn from their sinful ways. America is no different and neither is the American church. The Lord is calling us to return to holiness and return to His Word, because if we repent and turn from our wickedness God will heal our land.

> . . . if my people, who are called by my name, will humble themselves and pray and seek my face and turn from their wicked ways, then will I hear from heaven, and will forgive their sin and will heal their land.
>
> 2 Chronicles 7:14 (NIV)

God doesn't say that if everyone in our country repents He will heal our land. God says, " . . . if my people, which are called by name." If pastors, teachers, preachers, and Christians of all kind will humble themselves and pray and seek His face and turn from their wicked ways, He will hear us from heaven, forgive our sins, and heal our land. God will not heal our land until we once again preach against sin. Many pastors across this country need to pray and ask forgiveness because they have let their pulpits be reduced to self-esteem clinics and turned the church into social clubs and houses of entertainment. They have become houses without correction and without reproof.

What should we be standing against? We should stand against all idolatry and what I call "modern Baal worship" in our country. The three basic tenets of Baal worship are this: child sacrifice, sexual immorality, and worship of animals and creation. We legally sacrifice children at the altar of convenience in murder camps called abortion clinics. The fact that we as the church of God are not completely outraged by this and don't rebuke our culture regularly for these atrocities just shows how cold our hearts have truly grown. Ten times more babies have been killed in the comfort of an air conditioned and legal abortion clinic than Jews that were slaughtered by Hitler in Nazi concentration camps. God, forgive our nation for exterminating precious lives that You created because we think our lives are too important to be bothered with a baby.

I have witnessed those who shy away from talking about the sin of abortion and many other sins that are political hot buttons, because they say they would rather talk about the love, mercy, and forgiveness of God. But once again let me remind you that Christ will not forgive you for a sin that you don't acknowledge. The beauty about preaching the truth is that it leads people to repentance. Instead of pretending like there is no sin, we should be preaching about sin so that people will feel conviction from the Holy Spirit and come to repentance. We have abandoned holiness to reach the world, but without holiness and a set-apart life in Christ we will not see God, nor will we be able to reflect God. Instead of minimizing sin we should preach the holiness and justice of God. It is in light of truth that we present an honest view of the love and mercy of God as displayed in the gospel.

The second tenet of Baal worship is sexual immorality. We are a culture immersed in immorality. It's everywhere. We have become so used to it that we hardly notice it anymore. If you took someone in a time machine from the 1950s and transported them to today, they would be utterly shocked by the comparison of that culture and ours. Sexual immorality was around back then, but the difference is that today we celebrate it. Pop culture encourages young people to engage in sex with many different partners; we market everything from car insurance to candy bars with half naked women. The objectification of women through pornography is so commonplace that much of what was once called pornography now is normalized to the point that children watch it, and what is considered smut is so vile that nudity and images of intercourse don't qualify anymore. Homosexuality has been culturally accepted to the point that if you speak out against it you are called a bigot because this has become normal and acceptable behavior.

The next wave of wickedness comes in the form of transgenderism and now children are being dressed up like the opposite sex and paraded around at gay pride marches. Meanwhile we argue if men should be able to go into women's dressing rooms and restrooms if they are dressed like women. All the while, the American church is afraid to speak up because they don't want to be called judgmental, or upset false converts, or put the building project behind schedule.

I heard one preacher say that if God doesn't judge America, He would have to apologize to Sodom and Gomorrah. I'm not saying that, but let's be honest. The hand of judgment is already at the door and anyone who has ears let them hear. We are completely depraved, and God will not put up with sexual immorality forever. Don't confuse His mercy and His patience with tolerance or acceptance. One day, God's mercy and patience will give way to His justice.

The third tenet of Baal worship is worship of nature and animals. I believe in being good stewards of God's provision and His creation but the secular atheists of environmentalism go far beyond stewardship and has crossed into idolatry. It's a slap in the face to the Creator of the universe when we marvel at the beauty and vastness of the universe and pay no mind to the Creator of the universe.

Environmental extremism is a symptom of a culture that thinks that it can literally control what God has made and what only He can truly maintain. If the world had any less gravity we would drift off into space; if it had anymore gravity we would all be crushed from the weight of it. If the temperature of the human body goes up or down by as little as seven degrees, you would instantly die. Not only do some within our culture value animal life more than human life but in our weakness, we have tried to attach the origin of our species to mere created things rather than to the Creator of all things.

There is no reconciling the American culture to the gospel, the Scripture, or to God. We will sit under His wrath unless we begin to weep and wail and repent of our wickedness. The Scripture says that those who reject the truth are storing up wrath for themselves on the day of judgment but those of us who bear the title of pastor or teacher should realize this applies to those who suppress the truth as well.

The wrath of God is being revealed from heaven against all the godlessness and wickedness of people, who suppress the truth by their wickedness, since what may be known about God is plain to them, because God has made it plain to them. For since the creation of the world God's invisible qualities—his eternal power and divine nature—have been clearly seen, being understood from what has been made, so that people are without excuse.

> For although they knew God, they neither glorified him as God nor gave thanks to him, but their thinking became futile and their foolish hearts were darkened. Although they claimed to be wise, they became fools and exchanged the glory of the immortal God for images made to look like a mortal human being and birds and animals and reptiles.
>
> Romans 1:18-23 (NIV)

The only way we can ever break the yoke of sin that is destroying our country, the church, and our own hearts, is to repent and turn from wickedness. Freedom from sin is found in the gospel because it brings salvation to everyone who believes. Salvation happens when we become aware of our sin, repent, and surrender our lives to Christ. It's by faith and true belief in Him that we not only find salvation, but freedom from sin. Faith is knowing that we stand justified before God and will be held blameless for our sins. This is what is means when the Scripture says, "for in the gospel the righteousness of God is revealed" (Romans 1:17, NIV). When we preach a gospel without repentance, we have a gospel without a remedy for sin and if we don't deal with our sin, we will never see God because a holy God cannot coexist with sin. Christ as revealed in the gospel is the one and only remedy for sin.

> For I am not ashamed of the gospel, because it is the power of God that brings salvation to everyone who believes: first to the Jew, then to the Gentile. For in the gospel the righteousness of God is revealed—a righteousness that is by faith from first to last, just as it is written: "The righteous will live by faith."
>
> Romans 1:16-17 (NIV)

CHAPTER 10

A CHURCH BUILT WITH HUMAN HANDS

The biblical premise for the growth of the church of Christ is that we are preaching the gospel and making disciples. The perverted form that this has taken in America today is something else entirely. A good question to ask ourselves is, is what we do in the American church a good representation of what Christ intended when He instituted the church?

Most pastors rate the success of their church on two things: money and attendance. Is this what God calls success? Can we reconcile the current American church to the Scriptures and the teachings of Jesus? I have wrestled with this question most of my life as a believer. Of course, without even a second thought, most pastors would say, "Of course we can. No one is perfect, but we do our best."

I'm not condemning pastors. I know that being a true pastor and preacher of the gospel has special challenges in this day compared to years past in America. But when compared to the rest of the world, or the climate in which Jesus or the apostles preached in, we have to admit that the reason we feel it is hard is due to the fact that we have become comfortable and complacent.

The Bible says that church is for Christians, and that it is for the worship of God and discipleship of believers. I am all for outreach and evangelism but in an effort to make non-believers feel comfortable, we have done some anti-biblical and drastic things within the walls of our churches.

THE NUMBER ONE OBJECTIVE IS GROWTH

The lengths many modern churches are willing to go in order to gain people is staggering to me. In our corporate-driven age, we have let every level of the church be infiltrated by the systems and methods of man. Mega churches are told by consultants what gimmicks will attract people and they gladly oblige because we must get people in the door to be able to minister to them, right? Anything that stands in the way of numerical growth is cast to the side. Many modern evangelical churches have decided things like Sunday school, corporate prayer meetings, and systematic and expository Bible study are obstacles to growth, so they are taken out.

Short, encouraging topical sermons with lights, smoke machines, and state-of-the-art production and music are installed in the hopes it will hold the attention of the falsely-converted masses long enough to convince them to make a decision for Christ—of course while the lights are down, and no one is looking around. Many of these churches at one time were true churches where the gospel was preached and disciples were made but have now fallen to the weighty pressure of cultural relevance, the seeker-friendly model, and secular-growth schemes. Some churches have been created exclusively by and for this movement.

Do we believe that Word of God transforms lives? Do we believe that it is the Spirit that draws people to repentance? Do we believe Christ is enough? Then what have we done to the church? I know most people who are caught up in secular leadership models and the seeker-friendly model are well intentioned, but frankly that doesn't matter. The idea that it is our responsibility to grow the church is foolish and not found in the Scripture. We are to preach the gospel and live lives that honor God, and Christ, through the power of the Spirit, will build His church. If we build something that truly honors God, we should be excited about bringing people, but changing the culture of church to get people in the door is worldly and foolish.

He saith unto them, but whom say ye that I am? And Simon Peter answered and said, Thou art the Christ, the Son of the living God. And Jesus answered and said unto him, Blessed art thou, Simon Barjona: for flesh and blood hath not revealed it unto thee, but my Father which is in heaven. And I say also unto thee, that thou art Peter, and upon this rock I will build my church; and the gates of hell shall not prevail against it.

Matthew 16:15-18 (KJV)

Christ Himself will build His church through confession of faith in Christ as revealed by the Holy Spirit. Where in the Scripture did it say that we must do whatever it takes to get people to come and join the church? Paul never wrote an epistle to Timothy that said, "I'll be there to check on the church in a few months and I hope that attendance is up by then." I am not against the church growing. Of course, it is a beautiful thing when the numbers of the Kingdom of God grow, when the full counsel of God is preached, when you retain people who truly surrender their lives to Christ and become part of the family and community of God. But not all growth is good growth! If your church is growing because you provide entertainment, a coffee bar, and encourage people despite the sinful lifestyle they are living that is not good growth.

The truth in love is what we should give the world. If we think we can truly love people without giving the whole truth according to the Scripture we are not only deceiving them we are also deceiving ourselves. Who are we to think that we know better than God, or that we have something to offer the world beyond the true love of God as revealed in the Scripture?

The problem is that most within the American church think that they have the truth because they agree with the paper-thin gospel of accommodation and comfort preached from the pulpit each Sunday. Church has become watching movie clips and preaching the same repackaged sermons of encouragement week after week. Some churches that are not doing this would if they had the resources and ability to do so.

Immediately after Jesus performed the miracle where He fed five thousand men, not counting women and children, with seven loaves of bread and a couple pieces of fish, He literally had the largest crowd of His ministry which numbered in the thousands. It is at this point most of us would have planted a mega church and made many compromises to hold onto as many people as we could. Jesus had something else in mind. He turned to the crowd knowing that most of them were not true disciples of His and He spoke a message that cut deep to the true intentions of the masses thus separating His followers from false converts.

> And when he had called the people unto him with his disciples also, he said unto them, Whosoever will come after me, let him deny himself, and take up his cross, and follow me. For whosoever will save his life shall lose it; but whosoever shall lose his life for my sake and the gospel's, the same shall save it. For what shall it profit a man, if he shall gain the whole world, and lose his own soul? Or what shall a man give in exchange for his soul? Whosoever therefore shall be ashamed of me and of my words in this adulterous and sinful generation; of him also shall the Son of man be ashamed, when he cometh in the glory of his Father with the holy angels.
>
> Mark 8:34-38 (KJV)

By today's standards, Jesus was an utter failure as a pastor. He took a potential mega church of thousands down to a handful of people with one sermon. Now we have a lot of excuses why what Jesus said here doesn't apply to us or our culture. I hear arrogant people say that it takes something different to reach people than it did then, or that it takes a lot more to reach this generation than it did in previous ones. This is foolish. The prophets of the Old Testament, the apostles, and Jesus all had something in common with the way they preached. They spoke the truth with boldness. The problem isn't that people have changed, it's that what we consider success in the church has changed. Success to us means a lot of people in the seats and lots of money in the bank, bigger and bigger buildings, programs, and projects. Many pastors have come to grips with the pragmatic view that the end justifies the means. Most won't come out and say it, but we all know that if we preach funny and witty topical messages about things people want to hear, things that benefit them and benefit the church machine, everyone walks away happy.

What preacher has the conviction and courage to preach the truth as it is written in Scripture by the power of the Holy Spirit and not bow down to accommodate the wants of man? No preacher would actually say that he is ashamed of Jesus, but when we don't preach His Word, word for word, and let the Holy Spirit do His work, our actions tell the truth about our hearts. This is why the Scripture says, "How hard is it for the rich to inherit the kingdom of God?" People who have a lot in this world feel like they have a lot to lose.

How do these pastors prepare sermons? Is it lying prostrate on their faces before the Lord as they weep over their flock, their city, and the lost? Or do they hire consulting firms who give them data about every detail of what it takes to create a large church built with human hands? Or do they read books about secular leadership models, church growth, and what's trending in the culture? The fruit of this is evident all around in the large groups of people who come to be entertained, encouraged, and comforted and worship at the altar of self and pray that God fill in the gaps of their American dream.

God have mercy on us. Please forgive our blasphemy, break us once again until all of our want is lost in sight of Your heavenly gaze. Withhold from us the damnation of worldly happiness and restore us to the joy of our salvation.

SEEKER-FRIENDLY, DISCIPLE-FRIENDLY—NOT SO MUCH

I love outreach and evangelism, nothing is closer to my heart than preaching the gospel to the lost and seeing people truly come to Christ. But the idea of completely undoing the church to accomplish this is not a sound one, and it is also not biblical. The great commission says, "Go into the world and make disciples." It doesn't say change the church to accommodate the world and win people over through entertainment and a gospel of accommodation. In my opinion, the most damaging thing to happen in evangelical Christianity in the last fifty years is the seeker-friendly movement and all the secular things that have been born out of it.

It is a touchy thing to talk about this with some people because they feel you are judging them. Although I completely disagree with the idea of remodeling the structure of the church to make the lost feel comfortable, that doesn't mean that there are not God-loving, God-fearing Christians in these churches. Some churches have been slightly impacted by this methodology while others have been completely overtaken by it.

What do I mean by seeker-friendly? Let's be clear about this, I am not saying that I don't want the church to reach out to a lost and dying world, because I do. Outreach is important, but whatever we do to attract people to the church must give way to the gospel once they are in the church. I love being creative about outreach. I believe the ground at the cross is level and that no one is too dirty or far away to be touched by God. I am also not criticizing churches for a "come as you are" atmosphere. We should be welcoming and open to anyone who wants to hear the message of Christ, but we must present the full and true message of Christ. What I am talking about are secular systems for church growth that have no foundation in the Scripture, methods that actually cartel and edit the true message of the cross and the Bible, and the systematic removal of Bible study, sound doctrine, and preaching the full counsel of God.

I want the lost to be invited and welcomed into the church. I just want them to be met with the truth of the gospel when they get there, not a watered-down, powerless gospel. I am a former drug addict and graduate of the *Teen Challenge* program. I was the "dirty and the lost" and obviously there have been churches on the other side of the spectrum that have been resistant to the lost, having no sense of outreach or evangelism, and frankly are just legalistic. But the pendulum has swung far the other way in our day and age nearly to the level where it seems like anything goes. Where is the holiness without which no man will see God? Holiness is not the same thing as legalism.

Anytime we remove or purposefully edit Scripture for the sake of not being offensive or in the name of numerical church growth, we are not only out of line, but we are denying Christ. You might say that is a little extreme, but Christ Himself is the Word and if you believe the Scripture is inherent and God-breathed, then that's exactly what you are doing. These churches are built by secular methods with data and research that shouldn't matter in the house of God, but if you are desperately trying grow a church to match the size of your ego, this process has been proven to work.

Rick Warren, the pastor of Saddleback Church in Lake Forest, California one of the largest churches in America is one of the pioneers of this method. Other men, like Bill Hybels, founding pastor of Willowcreek Church in Chicago, Illinois, who went on to become megachurch pastors gained much of this corporate methodology by being mentored under a man by the name of Peter Drucker. Warren, who is probably the most famous in the seeker-friendly movement, has said no man has had more influence on his life and ministry than Peter Drucker.

Peter Drucker was an Austrian-born American management consultant, educator, and author, whose writings contributed to the philosophical and practical foundations of the modern business corporation. He had a brilliant business mind and made many positive contributions to society. Several pastors and Christian leadership gurus were mentored by and credit Drucker with having an impact on the seeker-friendly and purpose-driven church movement. Drucker taught these pastors to view potential church goers as customers and that to attract them we must market the product to them. The *product* being church. Give them entertaining services, with high tech production. Don't inconvenience them or ask too much of them. He taught them to remove things that got in the way of reaching the goal of gaining people and gaining contributions.

Don't misunderstand me. I am not opposed to mobilizing people for the sake of achieving social change and helping others. But this is not the church. It is a social club that raises money to help people while making them feel good about themselves and entertaining them. *Growth isn't the purpose of the church.*

The prophets didn't treat the people of the Old Testament like customers, and neither did Jesus or the apostles. They boldly, yet lovingly, preached the truth. Sometimes people repented and accepted it. Other times they threw rocks, tried to kill them, put them in prison, or ran them out of town. As for the church itself, the church is for believers who are part of the family of God to be discipled and, through the preached Word of God, conform to the image of Christ.

Peter Drucker to the best of my knowledge was not a born-again Christian and is widely reported as denying the divinity of Christ but felt that the American church could be impactful for philanthropy which was something he cared greatly about. He was famous for developing the corporate structure in American business and wanted to use those skills to mobilize the church for philanthropy. Although as Christians we should help those in need, we cannot be fooled into believing that this is the primary purpose of the church or that we can sacrifice fundamental truth for the sake of social change. Worshiping God, equipping the saints through God's Word, and preaching the gospel is the point of the church. Everything else is secondary and less important. The seeker-friendly model and purpose-driven model is secular and focuses on numerical and financial church growth rather than uncompromised truth and spiritual growth.

Rick Warren said that when he planted Saddleback Church he went around to all the homes in his city and began to ask if they belonged to a temple, mosque, or church. If they said yes, he said, "Thank you, sorry for bothering you, have a good day," and then he left. If they said no, he used a consulting questionnaire to ask them why. He wanted to know things like what kind of music they preferred? What is a good length for the service? Why they didn't attend church? What turned them off or offended them at church? And what he could do to get them to attend? This is insane!

Trying to get people to come to church is a good thing but changing the environment of church to make people stay is heresy. This has nothing to do with proclaiming the Scriptures and making true disciples. Building a church for the unconverted to make them feel comfortable doesn't sound much like, "Go into all the world and make disciples." Instead of telling them to have a good day when they said they were part of a mosque or temple, how about preaching the gospel to them?

HOW TO MAKE A SEEKER-FRIENDLY CHURCH

To make a seeker-friendly church grow you must do the following things:

Preach only upbeat and positive messages. Don't say or do anything that might offend or upset someone in the church. The idea of discipleship is completely contrary to this thought. People will call you judgmental or legalistic if you preach holiness or repentance from the pulpit, even if what you say is delivered in love and comes straight from the Bible. People want to hear things from the pulpit that communicate only these two things: you're important and you're okay.

Sunday service must be entertainment-driven. In order to get people's attention and keep them coming back, we must give them what they want. The goal is not to proclaim the truth of God's Word like the prophets did or the apostles did, but it is to get as many people in the seats as possible and to do whatever it takes to keep them there.

Replace the true gospel with a social gospel. Don't tell people that all have sinned and fallen short of the glory of God and apart from salvation through Jesus Christ they are headed down a broad road that ends in sure destruction.

Just tell them that God loves them no matter what and wants them to be successful and happy. Don't preach about sin or repentance or living a life of holiness. Focus solely on their felt needs; make sure they know church is about *them*.

Messages must be positive. Preaching must encourage the saved and unsaved alike. People or preachers who speak "negativity" have no place in the seeker-friendly church even if that negative statement is truth from the Scripture. There is no place for Paul's mandate to correct, rebuke, and encourage. All that's left is the seeker-friendly mandate to encourage no matter what. Every message is about giving in order to receive, bettering relationships, finances, moods, self-esteem, self-empowerment, and personal destiny. Dream big and God will make all of your dreams come true.

Remove anything that stands in the way of church growth such as Sunday school, prayer meetings, and expository preaching. All things that cause people to be bored must be expelled. Messages must be topical, witty, and short. Instead of calling it a *sanctuary* like in the Scripture, call it an *auditorium* which is much more neutral. Take out crosses and religious items or church related decorations that may cause "seekers" to get offended or feel uncomfortable. Remove anything that stands in the way of growth.

Remove systematic Bible study and preaching. If we dig deep into the Scripture not only will it bore people but also it creates unnecessary controversy, which is in opposition to growth. If someone within the larger congregation decides that they would like to systematically study the Bible, they have a small group that you can attend.

Any compromise you make in the name of church growth equals bad growth. It takes great pride and arrogance to believe that we have something to offer beyond Jesus, the Scriptures, and the gospel. It's the flesh that is gratified when we think that our human hands built something that the person of Christ was unable to build. This is why we are obsessed with growth—we care more about the short time in which we stand before man than the fact that one day we will give an account to God.

They use Scripture as a validator to try and add authority to the pragmatic messages they preach. Instead of preaching and proclaiming the Scripture and elaborating on it, they preach what's in their own minds, drawing from pop culture, secular psychology, philosophy, and even other religions to fashion messages that will be accepted by the masses.

Many of these men know the truth, but they muzzle it for the sake of church growth. A comedy routine accompanied by a few stories and a couple of Scriptures isn't proclaiming the Scriptures. The reason that it is so important to preach the Scriptures rather than only using the Scripture to prop up the message you want to preach is because we are human and humans typically take the path of least resistance. When we honestly work through the Scriptures it forces us to deal with things that we don't want to face. Dealing with issues and elements of our fallen nature isn't always easy, but that's what discipleship is. I'm not saying it's wrong to preach topical messages ever. I am saying that when that's all that is preached, it's easier to navigate around issues you would rather not face. This is at the core of the seeker-friendly method. We are mere undershepherds of the true Shepherd, Jesus Christ, and we will give account one day not for how big we built our church but for how true we stayed to the gospel.

THE SOCIAL GOSPEL

The term *social gospel* comes from a movement that gained prominence in the late nineteenth and early twentieth century in which Christian intellectuals aimed to use Christian ethics to solve problems such as war, poverty, social injustice, crime, and addiction. While trying to tackle these problems in and of itself is a good thing, it was the philosophy behind it that made it flawed. The people behind this movement focused solely on these issues while almost completely downplaying or altogether ignoring issues like true salvation, sin, heaven and hell, final judgment, and other important spiritual matters.

Salvation in the social gospel is about the here and now rather than eternal salvation which is granted to those who follow Christ and endure to the end. The greatest flaw of the social gospel is that it implies that the return of Jesus somehow hinges on our ability as humans to right all wrongs in the earth. True theology says the world will be imperfect until Jesus returns and at that time He will bring justice to the earth.

Jesus had compassion for the sick and hurting. He fed them, healed them, and forgave their sins, but He never got involved in politics nor did He mediate disputes. That was not the kind of justice He came to bring. He was not interested in social justice, He was interested in seeking and saving those who were lost.

Someone in the crowd said to Him, "Teacher, tell my brother to divide the inheritance with me." Jesus replied, "Man, who appointed me a judge or an arbiter between you?" Then He said to them, "Watch out! Be on your guard against all kinds of greed; life does not consist in an abundance of posses- sions." And He told them this parable: "The ground of a certain rich man yielded an abundant harvest. He thought to himself, 'What shall I do? I have no place to store my crops.'"

> "Then he said, 'This is what I'll do. I will tear down my barns and build bigger ones, and there I will store my surplus grain. And I'll say to myself, "You have plenty of grain laid up for many years. Take life easy; eat, drink and be merry.'" "But God said to him, 'You fool! This very night your life will be demanded from you. Then who will get what you have prepared for yourself?' "This is how it will be with whoever stores up things for themselves but is not rich toward God."
>
> Luke 12:13-21 (NIV)

As Christians we should be just and fair and treat people the way God would, but let us never confuse social justice with the gospel. Social justice is focused on a world that is quickly passing away, but the gospel is focused on the eternal soul of man and salvation through Jesus Christ.

In our day and age people are hungry to feel as if they are a part of some- thing greater. Many people use social media to speak out on social injustice from the comfort of their home rather than doing anything to solve the problems that face our world. But increasingly, there are many people who are willing to work towards goals and put their money where their mouth is. There are those who care enough to take action—not just Christians but people in general.

It is a good thing to care about the underprivileged, the poor, the hungry, and the oppressed. These are biblical concepts and we as Christians should live our lives in a manner that serves others, but let's not confuse this with the gospel. The gospel isn't about righting social wrongs, it is freedom from the yoke of sin and salvation through Christ by which we will spend eternity with Him. The idea of righting all social wrongs isn't the point of the gospel.

I'm not sure what will become of the great nation of America in the future, but I do know this: one day Christ will return and redeem those of us who have sworn allegiance to His kingdom. We will be transformed in the blink of an eye. The Kingdom of God won't be a democracy, it will be a theocracy which will truly be one nation under God and Christ will be king forever and ever.

> He will be great and will be called the Son of the Most High. The Lord God will give him the throne of his father David, and he will reign over Jacob's descendants forever; his kingdom will never end."
>
> Luke 1:32-33 (NIV)

I believe that our democratic republic is the best possible system of government in a world that is awaiting the return of its King, but the only thing that sets us apart as a nation is the fact that we have a right to freely and openly worship God. The origins of our nation are uniquely God-centered and everything from our laws to our system of government were designed to honor God and give freedom to man who was created in His image. But as we have given ourselves over to sin, idol worship, and depravity, the very nature of God's blessing on this nation has begun to unravel. Without repentance we will not escape the judgment of the Lord.

The idea of loving your neighbor as yourself is a noble one but it falls short of the greatest good, which is to love the Lord your God with all of your heart, soul, and mind. Loving others and doing what is right toward them isn't the highest aim; it is merely a by-product of God's love for us. Many within the modern church have made it seem like social issues are the highest aim of the church. Helping others is important but if you do this and don't preach the true gospel, you are doing no good. Nothing is more important than drawing sinners to repentance by preaching the true gospel to a lost and dying world. If you feed people and help people while presenting the gospel to them, you are using goodness to glorify God, but if the gospel isn't attached to your benevolence you are merely bringing glory to yourself.

The idea that the gospel is a means to fight all social injustice in the world is a false one. Before we are saved, or when we are new to the faith, we show our immaturity because we think everything is about us. Our worldview and perspective is one of "self." We always consider how things affect us before we consider others or God.

The next level is a view that puts others before ourselves but still considers others' needs or feelings before God. Although this seems better it is still a flawed order of priorities. It is the reason many within the church have softened towards homosexuality and abortion, and put people's feelings before God's feelings. It is because they have the two greatest commandments out of order. It is wrong to put people before God. Our love for people should flow out of our love for God not the other way around. If we think that telling people that God doesn't have a problem with a lifestyle of sin, or that God loves them too much to judge them, we are lying to them and to ourselves.

> Jesus replied: "'Love the Lord your God with all your heart and with all your soul and with all your mind.' This is the first and greatest commandment. And the second is like it: 'Love your neighbor as yourself.'; All the Law and the Prophets hang on these two commandments.
>
> Matthew 22:37-40 (NIV)

Jesus tells us what He expects from us in the words of Scripture. How we *feel about this* is inconsequential. The way we love people and how we prioritize what's important in our life should come from the Scripture. What is socially in fashion at the time should never change this fact; we must put God first, others second, and ourselves last if we want to live a life that pleases God.

Today much of the church seems to think that being benevolent is the gospel, and while we should always be benevolent we should do this *in addition to* preaching an uncompressed gospel message. If we don't we are just sending well-fed people to their destruction.

We have been conditioned to believe that what the world views as success, and what God considers success, is the same thing. That simply is not true. God is looking for Daniels to thrive in Babylon as holy men and women of God, not for people to become Babylonian in order to gain the culture's acceptance. If we truly believe that God is impressed by gains we make in our compromise, then we are more blind than the people we are trying to save.

We cannot build Christ's church by compromising His message, withholding His truth, or editing or watering down His words. Corrupt human hands can never build the church of Christ. We are mere laborers who work in His vineyard and execute His will. Nothing we do to complete our vision by our will and through secular methods pleases God. What pleases God is when His servants and anointed messengers preach and proclaim His Word fearlessly and with conviction, trusting that when the gospel is preached under the anointing of the Spirit, hearts will be changed.

Men construct buildings and organizations, but only Christ through His supernatural power will build His church and the gates of hell will not prevail against it. Churches built with secular methods, by human hands, will not prevail against anything. Just like a house built on the sand, it will not endure the test of time, and neither will their deeds endure the fire by which Christ will try all things. On that day all things built with human hands will be burned up, but what Christ builds upon Himself will surely endure forever.

CHAPTER 11

HEALING THROUGH REPENTANCE

Throughout the Scriptures, when the judgment of God fell on Israel, He would look throughout the land not for a strong man, a smart man, or even a wise man. He looked for a praying man, a man who was grieved by sin the same way He was, who strived to live righteously and longed for the holiness of God. Some people like to talk only about the wrath of God. On the other side of the spectrum there are many more who focus on and talk about only the love of God. While both are true and are real attributes of God, there is only one attribute of God that is so important it's mentioned more than any other in the Scripture, and when it is mentioned often it is repeated three times in a row to show its importance. This attribute is *His holiness*.

> And they were calling to one another: "Holy, holy, holy is the Lord Almighty; the whole earth is full of his glory."
>
> Isaiah 6:3 (NIV)

America is not beyond saving but God's salvation and restoration isn't offered to the arrogant and the prideful; it is only extended to the contrite and repentant. We are in desperate need of God's mercy and grace, but what most think that means is something far from the reality that is presented to us in Scripture. Praying for God's blessing and favor will not undo what we face in this nation. Only a heart of repentance and a church that is willing to once again seek God's face and mourn our sin and turn from wicked ways will. Don't we know that it was God's holiness that required a payment for sin in the first place? God doesn't just hate sin, He cannot have sin in His presence. Here in our hedonistic culture, full of filth and depravity, we think we are doing good by sinning less. What we fail to realize is the fact that God can never accept sin. Although we will never be perfect this side of heaven, believing that because Christ died for us we shouldn't worry about sin is as foolish as saying because I'm an imperfect husband I shouldn't strive to be faithful to my wife. She said till death do us part so why does it matter if I cheat? She is required to forgive me, right? Just because God made a way for us to stand righteous before Him through the blood of Christ, doesn't mean everyone will benefit from this, only those who in humility bow deep before Him in surrender and repentance.

I fear that many who are now asleep to the mixture that has crept into the church will not be easily awakened. Have you ever heard the old story about cooking a frog in a hot pot of water? It is a crude and simple story but the point it communicates is direct and concise. If you throw a frog into a boiling hot pot of water he will jump out as soon as the scolding water touches his skin because it is shocking and painful. But if you put a frog into a lukewarm pot of water and slowly began to increase the temperature little by little the frog will let you boil it alive. It doesn't feel the pain or shock of the heat because he is getting used to the temperature little by little and once it's hot enough to boil him it is too late.

What about the church—homosexual clergy, rejection of the Bible, worldly music, systems and methods, no altars, no crosses, no Bible study, no real prayer, sin accepted on every level, sound doctrine replaced with the witty but empty words of man, holiness now called legalism. But because we have become used to sin and depravity, little by little we find ourselves now at the boiling point. So where do we start? It's not in our culture or even in the church. The place we must start is in our own hearts and in our own lives.

When we earnestly pray and seek God, He will refine us and work out the impurity in our lives. Healing starts with repentance! I know many Christian people who live carefree lives and feel as if they have arrived and that they have reached a state of grace that no longer requires repentance. I fear for these people the most.

Why are they not concerned with the holiness of God? Why don't they lament and mourn over sin? Why doesn't the thought of their lost loved ones drive them to a prayer closet? Why aren't we fearlessly proclaiming the gospel and preaching salvation through the repentance of sin secured by Christ's shed blood? The prophets did, John the Baptist did, Jesus did, and the apostles did. What makes us think we have transcended the need for prayer and repentance? Maybe it's because we are no longer true students of the Scripture, nor do we live lives that are consumed with prayer. When you talk like this nowadays people say you are legalistic. In some corrupt circles of men, a husband might be ridiculed for being faithful to his wife, or because he won't watch pornography, or go to topless bars, or pick up women for one-night stands. Be wary of people who claim to love God but like to argue for and explain away sin. From the abundance of the heart the mouth will speak.

How can we look out across the church of entertainment and compromise and not mourn? It's because we have built a home in this world and decided to have our best life now, instead of living like pilgrims, foreigners, and exiles who are only passing through. Our mission is to preach the gospel and live lives of righteousness that far exceed that of the Pharisees and the teachers of the law, living as salt and light in a tasteless and dark world. People who believe that God's grace should make us less concerned with striving towards holiness truly don't understand the nature of an intimate relationship built on love and trust.

> Dear friends, I urge you, as foreigners and exiles, to abstain from sinful desires, which wage war against your soul. Live such good

lives among the pagans that, though they accuse you of doing wrong, they may see your good deeds and glorify God on the day he visits us.

1 Peter 2:11-12 (NIV)

The perversion of grace that has taken hold over much of the church almost makes it seem like you are doing something wrong if you actively work to abstain from the sinful desires that are waging war against your soul. But please remember Matthew 7:13-14 where it says broad is the road that leads to destruction. God's grace does cover us, but if you still love sin and the things of this world you should probably look around and see if your surroundings are broad and if the road you walk is broad. Are you going with the flow and moving with the masses or are you on a narrow path fenced in with sound doctrine? Living a life like the Apostle Peter says makes you stand out from the crowd. Does your life look a lot like those outside the faith or are you known for living a life of holiness and a life of Christ-like love?

Therefore, since we have these promises, dear friends, let us purify ourselves from everything that contaminates body and spirit, perfecting holiness out of reverence for God.

2 Corinthians 7:1 (NIV)

I'm convinced that people who love God will strive for holiness because of the inner working of the Holy Spirit. Why do we pervert grace to mean something it doesn't? Grace doesn't mean do what you want, grace means since we are in fellowship with a perfect and holy God, we need grace to exist. Those who truly love God will strive for holiness and live lives that bring glory to the name of Jesus. When we fall, grace is there to draw us to repentance and for those who repent, God is faithful to forgive. But people who don't feel the need to live in repentance either have no sin, which is impossible, or reject God's true grace through their pride.

But He gives more grace. Therefore, He says: "God resists the proud, But gives grace to the humble."

James 4:6 (NKJV)

It is interesting to hear people who seek to excuse a life of compromise and, in their pride, call this the grace of God. They get upset when you speak about striving for holiness or purifying ourselves from things that contaminate our body or spirit. But Paul, the person who wrote more than any other biblical writer about the grace of God, also wrote often about separating ourselves from sin and living lives of repentance. He never used grace as an explanation or excuse for sin. On the contrary, he used terminology like, "beating his flesh into subjection and self-denial for the sake of God's glory." You often find when you discuss these issues with people who resist the idea of repentance, they use terminology like "I feel like," and "I believe God means," but rarely will you hear a direct statement like "the Bible says."

When we spend time in His presence and in His Word, not devotionals, not books about His Word, not listening to feel-good topical messages, but reading His Word line upon line, and precept upon precept, we begin to see things His way. Spending time in His presence will draw us to repentance because how can you be in the presence of a holy God and not feel like the prophet Isaiah did:

"Woe to me!" I cried. "I am ruined! For I am a man of unclean lips, and I live among a people of unclean lips, and my eyes have seen the King, the LORD Almighty."

Isaiah 6:5 (NIV)

Have we surpassed the prophet Isaiah? We live in compromise and in a culture so depraved that our eyes are exposed daily to things that stain our very soul and you're telling me that being in the presence of God doesn't draw us to repentance? How can we be in God's presence and not be in frightful awe? The fear of the Lord is the beginning of wisdom. Some might say that was the Old Testament and we now have a different relationship with God because of Christ. In some ways this is true, but I don't think that changes what a sinful man feels when he comes into the presence of a Holy God.

Let us consider John the apostle. No disciple had a closer and more dear relationship with Jesus than John, the son of Zebedee. In his gospel he refers to himself as the disciple whom Jesus loved. It says in the Scripture that John rested his head upon Jesus' chest; he would have been close enough to hear the very heartbeat of the Savior. John was as close to Jesus as any human ever was, but when he came in contact with the resurrected Christ in all His glory in the book of Revelation, it says that the glory of God was so great on Jesus that when John saw Him he was terrified and fell at his feet as if he was a dead man.

> When I saw him, I fell at his feet as though dead. Then he placed his right hand on me and said: "Do not be afraid. I am the First and the Last."
>
> Revelation 1:17 (NIV)

Spending a lot of time in His presence will keep us reverent toward God, living in repentance, and striving towards holiness. If we begin to fast and pray and seek God's face, He will heal our calloused hearts; He will break our hearts of stone and give us hearts of flesh. Then we will care less and less about the trappings and toys of this world. We have a choice to repent of our infidelity toward God, to divorce ourselves from the world and all it has to offer, and to pledge our faithfulness to the bridegroom who has redeemed us, or embrace this world and reject the Lord. You can't have both. If you love the world or the things of this world, the love of God is not in you!

> Do not love the world or anything in the world. If anyone loves the world, love for the Father is not in them. For everything in the world—the lust of the flesh, the lust of the eyes, and the pride of life—comes not from the Father but from the world. The

world and its desires pass away, but whoever does the will of God lives forever.

1 John 2:15-17 (NIV)

If we do the will of God we will live forever, because of what Christ has done for us. The lust of the flesh, the lust of the eyes, and the pride of life are in opposition to a surrendered servant of Jesus. Stay pure, resist the traps the enemy has built to entice your sinful nature—put it to death by starving it out.

We can no longer let our culture set the standard for what is acceptable and what is right. We must work out our own salvation with fear and trembling before the Lord. We must search out our deceitfully wicked hearts according to the Scripture and put to death anything that doesn't pass the test. Personal holiness is what we must work toward. It's up to Christ to take the life that we have given as an offering to Him and transform it from the inside out, but it's up to us to deny ourselves, pick up our cross, and follow Him.

We must pray with reverence and humility because this is the kind of prayer God wants from us. A man that has no sense of remorse for his sin has no place with God. How can we enter the temple with pride in our step and arrogance in our heart unless we are deceived? A man aware of his sin, is a man who knows he needs God's mercy. This is living in repentance. Heaven will be full of these kinds of people because only people who are truly aware of their desperate need for God will approach Him in humility.

> "Two men went up to the temple to pray, one a Pharisee and the other a tax collector. The Pharisee stood by himself and prayed: 'God, I thank you that I am not like other people—robbers, evildoers, adulterers—or even like this tax collector. I fast twice a week and give a tenth of all I get.'
> "But the tax collector stood at a distance. He would not even look up to heaven, but beat his breast and said, 'God, have mercy on me, a sinner.'

"I tell you that this man, rather than the other, went home justified before God. For all those who exalt themselves will be humbled, and those who humble themselves will be exalted."

Luke 18:10-14 (NIV)

HEALING FOR THE CHURCH AND OUR NATION

What we must do first and foremost is realize that the church isn't every group of people who gather together on Sunday. The remnant, or the true church, was established and is built and sustained by the person of Jesus Christ. Where should we gather together? The first question you should ask is this: is the Word of God preached and proclaimed from the pulpit? If the answer is no, turn around and look for a church where it is. Does the Scripture have the final say in all situations? Does the Scripture have the authority? None of that other stuff matters. There's nothing wrong with having a great sound system or an amazing children's program, but not at the expense of sound doctrine.

Obviously, nothing touched by human hands can be perfect, but if a church doesn't seem to be deeply concerned with what the Scripture says about all things, then find a church that does. Watch out for celebrity preachers. I am not saying that all notable or popular teachers are bad, I am simply saying make sure you judge a tree by its fruit. Don't trust someone just because they are famous. In fact, be more skeptical. Is Jesus the star or is a man? The job of a preacher is to simply proclaim the word of God, anything beyond that is from the evil one.

The American church needs to repent for falling so far. We must rebuke false teachers and hold people who say they represent Christ to the standard of the Scripture and God will honor this. He always has. This is what the prophets of Old Testament looked like, this is what the preachers and apostles of the first century church looked like, and this is what we should be doing as well. We must destroy all the idols and raise up a standard that brings glory to God and lays our flesh to waste. We must decrease so Christ can increase in us.

Healing in the church, or in a nation, always starts with a few who are faithful. People like Nehemiah who was willing to rebuild the wall around Jerusalem with one hand building the wall, and the other hand holding a sword. In the story of Nehemiah, Israel was in ruin and the wall that protected the great city of Jerusalem was in rubble.

Nehemiah was the cupbearer for the Artaxerxes, king of Persia. As the cupbearer, Nehemiah lived in the palace and probably had a comfortable life. He became aware that there was trouble for his countrymen because they were exposed without the wall of protection around the city. God called Nehemiah to go and rebuild the wall. Things probably looked beyond repair but God called and Nehemiah obeyed. He was called by God to risk all his worldly comfort and to ask the king's permission to rebuild the wall of his homeland, which the king allowed. But once he began the process of rebuilding the wall, he faced trial and opposition of all kinds. Nehemiah was a man of patience, courage and integrity, a man of true conviction, but most importantly he was a man of prayer. He waited for an answer from God for months while fasting and praying about how to proceed to recover this ruined situation. He was persecuted greatly by Sanballat and Tobiah while trying to rebuild the wall. These men tried to stop him through sabotage, and they scoffed at his attempts. They threatened to injure or kill the men working with him as well as threatening to kill Nehemiah himself. But nothing could stop him, nothing could cause him to waver. He had heard from God, and would trust God and do the work God had called him to do.

We find ourselves in a similar situation here as Christians in America. Men who have grown fat and comfortable in Persia and would rather be cupbearer to the king of this world than to stand for the truth and rebuild the wall. We need pastors and preachers of conviction who cannot rest until the wall is rebuilt—men of true faith who are willing to follow the conviction of what God spoke to them even if that leads them to persecution or death. We need preachers who preach like prophets, who preach like apostles, who preach like Jesus. Whatever happened to praying through? Whatever happened to waiting on the Lord until He moves? Where are the men and women of God who will rebuild and watch the wall? God is looking for humble but bold men and women who want to hear from God so desperately they will fast and pray until He shows Himself. Lead us through the narrow gate of repentance, Lord. Break us once again, so You can build us back into something that is pure and holy and brings glory to Your name.

In 1 Kings 18:16-45, the prophet Elijah found himself in a similar situation. Because of Israel's wickedness, they were under God's judgment and Elijah prayed and God withheld the rain for three and a half years. At the same time Jezebel who was the wife of King Ahab was killing the prophets of the Lord. She had turned the people to idol worship and to living in all sorts of wickedness. The people then, much like in our culture, claimed to serve God, but they also worshiped Baal and Asherah. This situation seemed almost unrecoverable because the entire nation was corrupted by sin and only a few true prophets of the Lord remained. But Elijah stood up and challenged the corruption and had faith that God would back him up. When you have truly sought the Lord and know you are in His will you can be confident that He will back you up. Like Elijah we must wait on the Lord. This is where most of a man or women of God's life is lived, on our knees in prayer. There is no better place than in His presence.

Basically, Elijah told the four hundred prophets of Asherah and the four hundred and fifty prophets of Baal to meet him on Mt. Carmel and they would both bring a bull to the mountain top and pray to their god and whoever's god answered by fire and consumed the bull was the true god and should be worshiped alone. Before Elijah does this, he makes a plea to the people.

Elijah went before the people and said, "How long will you waver
between two opinions? If the LORD is God, follow him; but if
Baal is God, follow him." But the people said nothing.

1 Kings 18:21 (NIV)

He preached a message of repentance before he called on God to rain
fire from heaven. This also a prophetic message for post-Christian America:
"How long will you waver between two opinions? If the Lord is God follow
Him, but if the idol of American dream is God, follow it. If the idol of entertainment is God, follow it. If money is God, follow it. Just remember to
choose wisely because you cannot serve two masters."

The story goes on and the prophets of Baal and Asherah laid their bull
on the altar and began to chant and dance for hours and nothing happened.
Then Elijah rebuilt the altar of the Lord laid his sacrifice on it and had them
pour several barrels of water on his sacrifice and then he prayed to the Lord.
The Lord sent fire from heaven and the Scripture says that it licked up all the
water and consumed the bull. After this the people fell on their face said
that the Lord is God. They gathered up the false prophets and killed them
all. Then Elijah prayed that rain would fall once again, and it did.

The drought was ended, and God let the blessing of His rain come
down but not before a couple of things happened. First, He called a man by
the name of Elijah who responded to the call of God. It's hard to respond
to the call of God in wicked culture when even the godly seemed to have
compromised. Second, Elijah responded to the call of God and in obedience preached repentance to the people. He stood up in the face of corruption and compromise and called out the wickedness of his generation.

Elijah wasn't seeker-friendly; he called the people to repentance. Third,
He rebuilt the altar of the Lord that the modern people of His generation
had torn down to pursue a religion of compromise. The altar represents
prayer and worship dedicated to a Holy God. Fourth, he poured out water on
the altar which in Israel was a precious resource because it is a desert land

and because they were in the middle of a drought. This proved that all his faith was in the one true God to come like fire and receive his offering. God showed up and the people fell on their faces in repentance. And finally, Elijah prayed that God once again would let in rain and it did.

Elijah stood up and rebuked the wickedness of the false prophets. There is no room for cowards in God's kingdom. Either you are for Him or you are against Him. You can't be both. There is no middle ground. Just like in our culture, when you truly stand up for Jesus it might be just you standing alone, but this is the faith it takes to see God move. If you are more worried about the opinion of man than the opinion of God than you probably don't know and fear God in wisdom as you should.

> "I tell you, my friends, do not be afraid of those who kill the body and after that can do no more. But I will show you whom you should fear: Fear him who, after your body has been killed, has authority to throw you into hell. Yes, I tell you, fear him."
>
> Luke 12:4-5 (NIV)

Just like the prophets of Baal and Asherah, the scientist who preaches evolution, the secular atheist, the academic elite, pop culture, and the church of entertainment and compromise, have no power to back up their claims. They may have a lot of followers with loud voices and a great marketing campaign, but they will never bring be able to deliver what the Lord can. How do we affect change that brings true repentance in the modern church and in our nation?

Rebuild the altar of the Lord: Before we can do anything else we must rebuild the altar of prayer that has been torn down to make room for a religion of comfort, compromise, worldly entertainment, and the idol worship that revolves around self. Elijah rebuild the altar of the Lord and laid out twelve stones to remind them of the true God who established Israel. He wanted to make sure that the glory for what was about to happen could be explained only by God. It's ironic that most churches in our day and age have taken out the altars and crosses, prayer meetings, and Bible study to make room for entertainment and useless babbling much like the prophets of Baal. Without earnest prayer and the preaching of the gospel, our churches are powerless and pointless.

Pour everything out on the altar: After Elijah rebuild the altar of the Lord, he laid his sacrifice on it just like the prophets of Baal and Asherah did, but he took it much further. He had them pour water over the sacrifice and over the altar, and in a trench that was dug around the altar. He didn't want them to have any room to say the fire came from any other place. God will do the impossible if you set the stage for Him to get all the glory. Remember it had not rained in three and a half years and Israel is a place where water was scarce anyway. Imagine the anger the people must have felt when the same guy who prayed that it wouldn't rain for three and a half years now is taking such a precious resource and pouring it all out on the altar. It reminds me of the story of the lady who broke the alabaster jar of very expensive oil to anoint the feet and head of Jesus and the anger it says the disciples felt because of this. She saw the value of the Lord and bringing glory to Him just like Elijah did. Jesus is worth it all. All things are for His glory including our lives, our time, and our resources; He deserves it all. It is when everything we have is laid out on the altar that God moves in power.

Pray for Fire: We have replaced the fire and power of God with the methods of man, complacency, and a religion of self. Why does it seem like a poor and persecuted church is the place God always seems to manifest His power? God has no weapon in this earth more powerful than a Spirit-filled disciple who is completely unpossessed by possession, loving nothing in this world but God and those created in His image. In the book of Acts, Peter walked past a lame man who is begging for money and Peter says to him, "Silver or gold I do not have, but what I do have I give you. In the name of Jesus Christ of Nazareth, walk" (Acts 3:6, NIV). And the lame man got up and walked away. This is the power of a church that burns with the fire and power of God where everything is poured out on the altar for His glory. Later in church history when the Catholic church had become rich, comfortable, and corrupt, St. Thomas Aquinas made a profound statement to Pope Innocent II regarding the wealth of the church and what price they had truly paid to become a rich church.

Aquinas entered the presence of Innocent II, before whom a large sum of money was spread out. The Pope said, "You see, the Church is no longer in that age in which she said, 'Silver and gold have I none.'" "True, holy father," replied Aquinas; "neither can she any longer say to the lame, 'Rise up and walk.'"

We find ourselves in a similar situation in the American church: we are rich but spiritually powerless. It is only when we pour out what we consider valuable that God sends fire from heaven. I'm not just talking about money, although our culture of excess is part of the problem. I'm talking about everything. God will not share His glory with a man, a church, an organization, with anything or anyone. God's healing for a person, for the church, or for our nation is found only on the other side of repentance. If we humble ourselves and repent of our infidelity, God will heal our land.

> . . . if my people, who are called by my name, will humble themselves and pray and seek my face and turn from their wicked ways, then I will hear from heaven, and I will forgive their sin and will heal their land. Now my eyes will be open and my ears attentive to the prayers offered in this place. I have chosen and consecrated this temple so that my Name may be there forever. My eyes and my heart will always be there.
>
> 2 Chronicles 7:14-16 (NIV)

The Scripture doesn't say that if everyone will humble themselves and pray and seek His face and turn from their wicked ways. Instead, it says if those *who are called by my name* will humble themselves and seek my face and turn from their wicked ways I will hear from heaven and heal their land.

The people of God through prayer, repentance, and seeking God can bring healing to the land. It starts with us. But God won't honor our self-centered, entertainment-driven, self-empowering prayer and worship. We must once again let Him break us and mold us for His intents and purposes, not ours. God will not set a life aflame that is not completely surrendered to Him and laid out on the altar.

It is impossible to reconcile the cost of discipleship and the gospel with the American dream of comfort, worldly success, and excess. We are to live as foreigners and exiles who are merely working in the vineyard and waiting for our master's return. We can lie to ourselves and comfort our seared consciences, but it is only in brokenness that God will accept us. The sovereign God of the universe became man to live, die, and rise again for us. Not so that we could become fat and comfortable in this sin-filled world, but so that we could endure and persevere through this world to be with Him forever in eternity.

When you think about eternity does it excite you? Is that what you are looking forward to? Or are you so comfortable in this life that you rarely think about, or long for, eternity? In the end, do you love Jesus and desperately long for His appearing like a wife whose husband has been away on a long journey? Are you trying to keep things in order in preparation for His return?

What sets America apart from the rest of the world is freedom, which is our greatest asset. But many Christians have hidden behind this freedom and have fallen into a deep sleep. Unfortunately, because of this, the spirit of antichrist has infiltrated our culture and the day will soon be upon us when we might have to stand for Christ in persecution beyond mere ridicule.

God did not send His Son into the world to condemn the world but that through Him the world could be saved. But to fully and honestly preach the gospel we must talk about sin, repentance, and hell, as well as love, grace, and mercy. The gospel isn't an American gospel, it is an eternal gospel.

Although we need to pray for our leaders and our country that God would have mercy on us and bring repentance and revival, we must also remember that our time here is short, and our citizenship is not of this country or even of this world. We are the sons and daughters of the Most High where heaven is our home.

The gospel and the true cost of being a disciple of Jesus will never reconcile to the American culture or whatever that culture says is the American dream. True preachers are messengers of warning. They preach a message that calls for man to be conformed to the image of Christ. We must preach the message of the prophets, the message of John the Baptist, the message of the Apostles and the message of Jesus: "Repent for the kingdom of God has come near!"

The people of the American church are starving for the word of truth to be preached with integrity and conviction. We need men and women of holiness to stand up and speak the truth without a thought of what it will cost them. We need a display of the power of the Holy Spirit to bring conviction that will once again lead us to repentance for the salvation of our souls. Nothing else matters my friends, and the hour is getting late. How long will we waver between two opinions? Either everything Jesus spoke in Scripture is true, including the teachings that are hard to accept, or none of them can be trusted. Either He is the God, or He is not. Either the Scriptures are true, or they are not. If they are not, then let's not waste anymore of our time discussing them. But if they are true and Jesus is Lord of all, then nothing else matters.

If we gain everything we want: full churches, with full bank accounts and everyone is enjoying their best life now, but we misrepresented Jesus or His words to accomplish it, we have gained nothing except judgment for ourselves. To create and worship an image of Jesus that is not firmly rooted in the Scriptures but one that we can accept is idolatry and to share this false Christ with others is blasphemy. God is full of love and rich in mercy, He will forgive us, but His forgiveness is found only on the other side of repentance. Seek the Lord while He may be found.

For what shall it profit a man, if he shall gain the whole world, and lose his own soul? Or what shall a man give in exchange for his soul?

> Whosoever therefore shall be ashamed of me and of my words in this adulterous and sinful generation; of him also shall the Son of man be ashamed, when he cometh in the glory of his Father with the holy angels.
>
> Mark 8:36-38 (KJV)